HELPING TO HEAL

The Arts in Health Care

Peter Senior and Jonathan Croall

This reprint of 'Helping to Heal' is produced
with the support of
The Wellcome Foundation Ltd.

Wellcome

Published by Calouste Gulbenkian Foundation
London 1993

Peter Senior NDD, ATC, FRSA is director of Arts for Health in Manchester. While a Senior Lecturer at Manchester Polytechnic, he had over 15 years of experience as the founder and director of Hospital Arts, Manchester, arts consultant to the DHSS and member of both the Attenborough Committee of Enquiry into Arts and Disabled People and the Carnegie Council (to promote and monitor developments following the Attenborough Report). In 1987 he received a National Art Collections Award for his 'outstanding contribution to the visual arts'. Formerly a member of the Community Arts Panel of North West Arts and Chairman of their Environmental Arts Panel, he is founder director of Partnership Arts Ltd, the environmental art company. Currently, he is an adviser to the Arts Council of Great Britain's Per Cent for Art Steering Group.

Jonathan Croall is a freelance writer, journalist and consultant. He writes for a number of national newspapers on the arts, education, health and environmental issues. He is the author of several books, including *Don't Shoot the Goalkeeper, Neill of Summerhill, Don't You Know There's A War On?, Dig for History*, and a children's novel, *Sent Away*. He has edited *All the Best, Neill: Letters from Summerhill*, and *Good Earth-Keeping: Education, Training and Awareness for a Sustainable Future*. He has worked in book publishing with Cassell, Penguin, Oxford University Press, Writers and Readers, and Bedford Square Press. He is a former features editor of the *Times Educational Supplement*, and editor and co-founder of *Arts Express* magazine. He lives in Richmond, Surrey.

Contents

Wellcome in the community

"Wellcome is an international pharmaceutical company dedicated to the discovery and marketing of products that promote human health and the quality of life".

The last part of this mission statement describes equally well the purpose of those exploring and implementing the use of the Arts in Healthcare, and thus Wellcome shares an interest in the subject of this book. Its community affairs programmes focus on issues which are complementary to its innovative role in pharmaceuticals, and include health and disability care, education links and community projects. Wellcome's involvement through Peter Senior with 'Arts for Health' since 1991 recognises our mutual interest in improving healthcare and the quality of life.

Besides helping to initiate hospital projects, supporting 'Arts for Health's' Newsletter, and assisting promotion of the concept, Wellcome uses the atrium space at its head office for arts exhibitions which have a charitable and health connection.

Our association with 'Arts for Health' has convinced us of the healing benefits of the arts: and supporting the use of Art in Healthcare is now seen as a modest, but essential part of our community activity.

Ron Sutton
Community Affairs Department
The Wellcome Foundation Ltd, 160 Euston Road,
London NW1 2BP

Foreword

The Calouste Gulbenkian Foundation (UK Branch) is particularly pleased to assist the birth of this book. In these straitened days anything which expects a public or private subsidy is required to show the value of its contribution to society. The benefits which even modest arts projects can bring to places of healing are convincingly demonstrated in words and illustrations.

Recognition of this in the UK has been due, at times almost single-handedly, to Peter Senior working in Manchester and elsewhere. The initial steps were recorded in Peter Coles's *Manchester Hospitals' Arts Project* (Calouste Gulbenkian Foundation 1981). The Foundation has for several years also helped a number of individual initiatives (though these are no longer part of our current programme): most recently in 1989 we helped an artist-in-residence to support young people working creatively with the residents of a Glasgow home for mentally disadvantaged people, and the next year we supported an artist-in-residence for the Royal Victoria Hospital, Belfast. We have also been glad to assist the development of arts in hospices, through the Hospices Prints Project and Art in Hospices.

Further help from other trusts, donors or volunteers is still badly needed. For every St Mary's Hospital in the Isle of Wight, there are dozens of sad, tired buildings across the UK and elsewhere, unnecessarily dispiriting for their staffs and patients to be in. With the health service under the financial pressure it is today, it is unrealistic to expect medical budgets to spare funds for art. But if any reader has ever benefited from a hospital or health centre, here is one way in which she or he might like to express their thanks.

This book is a collaborative venture between Peter Senior and Jonathan Croall. The main chapters have been written jointly, but in certain cases, for example in chapters 1 and 2, where Peter Senior is narrating his own experience, it has seemed best for him to use the personal pronoun. The four case-studies were written by Jonathan Croall alone.

Ben Whitaker
Director
UK Branch
Calouste Gulbenkian Foundation

Chapter 1
Introduction

'It can't be easy to be healed in a soulless concrete box with characterless windows, inhospitable corridors and purely functional wards. The spirit needs healing as well as the body.'
The Prince of Wales, A Vision of Britain

The ancient Greeks saw a clear link between the arts and healing. At Epidaurus in the Peloponnese, the magnificent amphitheatre stands next to what was once the sanctuary of the god of healing, and a hospital. Here the sick and infirm would come from all over Greece, hoping for a cure. During their stay they would rest and take exercise, go on a diet and, as part of the healing process, walk across to the vast 14,000-seat theatre built into the nearby hillside, to attend a performance of a tragedy or comedy.

In many cultures the connection between the arts and health care has been a strong one in the past. In more recent times it has been largely lost sight of. In Britain initiatives have generally been confined to the visual arts. Most famously, in 1735 the artist William Hogarth painted a large mural for a staircase in St Bartholomew's Hospital in London, 'Christ at the Pool of Bethesda', which remains in place today. During the Victorian period attempts were made to brighten up some hospitals with works of art and craft; some of the beautiful decorative tiles of the time still survive. The nineteenth century also saw some early attempts to encourage artistic activity by patients.

In our own times a major landmark was the creation of the Paintings in Hospitals scheme in 1959. The idea came from Sheridan Russell, who was then almoner at the National Hospital for Nervous Diseases in Queen Square, London. For some time, both there and at the Maida Vale Hospital, he had been showing paintings by contemporary artists in waiting rooms, corridors and wards. The paintings had been lent by the artists, their owners, or private galleries, and appeared to interest patients and visitors in a way that the usual reproductions failed to do. The scheme grew rapidly, and today makes available its collection of some 1,400 works to over 80 hospitals and hospital departments in the London area and elsewhere.

The initiative provided an invaluable basis for wider consideration of the role of the arts in hospitals. But it is really only in the last two decades that the broader notion of the arts being a part of the healing process has begun to be seriously explored.

Few have put the case for such an idea more eloquently than John Davis, Professor Emeritus in paediatrics at the University of Cambridge. He suggests that art provides a way of coping with the whole of life, including disease and death. 'Art should not be seen as one of those activities like physiotherapy that is ancillary to medicine; nor as alternative medicine. It is concerned with our common sensibility, and our shared vision of what life is about, and how it should be lived...Art should help us in medicine to minister to patients as whole persons living out their lives, enabling us to treat life in its totality...Art, including the performing arts, has the power to reconcile us to the painful problems that life presents, its truths, and the suffering and sacrifices that it entails for so many people.' (1)

Today, a growing number of patients, doctors, consultants, nurses, therapists, architects, planners,

Early hospital art: Hogarth's celebrated painting 'Christ at the Pool of Bethesda', St Bartholomew's Hospital, London.

*Early decorative tiles in the Royal
Berkshire Hospital, Reading.*

health managers and other health care staff are
coming to recognise that, if the arts have a value in
society, they must have a special part to play in
places such as hospitals and hospices, where people
are facing unusual or distressing circumstances,
restricted movement, birth and death. The projects
and arts programmes that have been set up around
the UK over the past two decades have shown them
how the arts can provide for the basic human needs,
for beauty, humour, relaxation, harmony, and
spiritual uplift. The experience of these years has
also shown that the arts are capable of achieving a
great deal within the health care field.

Recently, in a health authority document, it has been
suggested that the arts can:

● 'Improve the quality of the health environment by
linking art, architecture and interior design·at every
opportunity;

● Present a positive image for the hospital or health
centre, displaying a cared-for appearance,
discouraging vandalism and encouraging a greater
sense of responsibility by all who use it;

● Orientate visitors, staff and patients when used as
an integral part of a directional signing system,
improving communications and traffic flow;

● Create closer links between local hospitals and
community groups, by involving them in activities
and events, thereby dispelling some of the
apprehension surrounding health care;

● Raise morale, inspiring confidence and self-
respect for both patients and staff, developing a

greater sense of responsibility and pride in the health
service;

● Assist patient recovery, alleviating stress and
boredom, providing reassurance and comfort,
humour and motivation, and giving purpose and
dignity to people's lives;

● Involve everyone, patients, staff and public,
enriching their lives inside and outside the health
care community.' (2)

It is of course very difficult to measure in any
scientific way claims made about the effect of the
arts and the visual environment on patient recovery.
Most of the evidence is anecdotal, such as that
offered by the pioneering nurse Florence Nightingale
in 1859: 'I have seen in fevers...the most acute
suffering produced from a patient (in a hut) not being
able to see out of the window, and the knots in the
wood being the only view. I shall never forget the
rapture of fever patients over a bunch of brightly
coloured flowers.' (3)

The Prince of Wales recently added his voice to the
debate when he suggested that positive qualities in
architecture, and in 'a sound healing or health care
environment', were in themselves 'health
promoting'. (4) There is plenty of anecdotal
evidence to support such a claim, some of which can
be found in this book. Many staff, some of them
initially dubious about the value of the arts for their
patients, have testified to the positive changes that
have occurred in their patients' or clients' behaviour,
as a result of improvements to their environment, or
their involvement in arts activities. John
Brocklehurst, professor of geriatric medicine at the
University of Manchester, spoke recently about the
value of arts activities within his region's health
services for the elderly: 'Studies have shown that
patients who participate gain much; they enjoy it;
they are evidently transformed in everyone's eyes
from patients into people; from a clinical point of
view we find that even the incontinence rate amongst
such patients falls.' (5)

Unfortunately scientific evidence to back up this
widespread view is in short supply. There is,
however, one study which is often quoted. In 1984
the researcher Roger Ulrich found that in one

hospital in the United States two dozen patients in a room with a window looking out on a natural scene had shorter post-operative stays, received fewer negative comments in nurses' notes, and required fewer doses of drugs, than a matching group whose windows faced a brick building. The differences between the two groups were significant, and provide useful back-up to what most people would consider an unsurprising result of such a comparison. (6)

There has as yet been no comparable independent research in the UK on this important question. There is, however, increasing evidence that planners and managers are reconsidering the question of the value of the environment for good health care. Recent changes within the National Health Service, where 'quality' is now supposed to be the watchword and 'putting the patient first' is high on the agenda, have certainly brought about a shift in approach. A health

service circular on quality assurance issued in 1989 stated: 'Public areas in hospitals in which patients wait should be pleasant, comfortable and visually attractive. Hospitals will have to provide plans for improving their appearance.'

The culture of the NHS is changing; the new system is making people look outwards. Some managers now see the arts as a useful means of creating a welcoming, user-friendly environment; others are using performing arts events or art workshops to demonstrate their concern for the 'whole' patient. There is more of an emphasis on new ideas;

Out-patients then and now: the London Hospital, Whitechapel 1910, and the Queen Elizabeth Hospital, Gateshead.

managers are being trained to be creative, to think laterally. At a time when they are more hard-pressed than ever, the forward-thinking ones are finding that the arts are providing them with all kinds of good ideas.

Nevertheless, there is still considerable resistance to change in many places. Lip-service may be paid to the value of landscaping and interior design by some health authorities, yet a great deal of education and persuasion needs to take place to convince them of the value of having a tree outside the window, a painting on the wall, or a mobile hanging from the ceiling. Institutional pressures can be strong, even where individuals within the institution may want to introduce changes involving the arts.

Money of course is one of the key constraints. The funding of arts programmes within health care is still a controversial and delicate matter. There are still plenty of people at all levels who regard arts programmes or works of art as a frivolous distraction, or at best a low priority for expenditure.

The changing NHS culture is bringing more emphasis on new ideas, exemplified by the high-tech, low-energy St Mary's Hospital in Newport, Isle of Wight.

Within a health service that is undergoing radical changes in organisation, convincing arguments need to be put forward to show that the introduction of a writer-in-residence, or a team of artists to create a mural along a bare corridor, will be cost-effective.

Mike Ruane, former general manager of the Central Manchester District Health Authority, recently stressed the need for support from key personnel: 'The funding of art in hospitals will always be a struggle for managers and artists alike...The most important ingredient for success is the commitment of individual managers to introducing some art into hospitals. Once that initial hurdle is overcome, the enthusiasm of patients and staff will propel it forward and make it easier to allocate funds...Once the intellectual acceptance of art in hospitals is achieved, managers and artists can and do display enormous ingenuity and effort in making things happen.' (7)

Until recently all funds for the arts in health care had to be raised from outside sources, so that they should not conflict with competing claims for health service revenue funds. This has meant that many energetic and creative people have been stifled in their

activities, spending too large a proportion of their time trying to get financial support for their work. In some places, however, once the value of the arts service has been appreciated by senior management, and by medical and nursing staff, it is increasingly being seen as a legitimate use of revenue funds. Some arts programmes have a proportion of their budget paid for from revenue funding, because it is seen as an important part of providing quality in patient care.

As will be seen from some of the projects and activities which feature in this book, the relationship between artists and health care staff may not always be an easy one, at least initially. To work as an artist in such situations it is necessary to be aware of the pressures, concerns and constraints of the jobs of the health care staff, and to get to know how the organisation works. Artists have to be educated to look at art in a different way. Too much of it is self-centred: artists are being trained who can't communicate at a basic level. Many are surprised to find, when they take up a residency, that the general public are intelligent and interested in the arts, and that knowledge and fresh ideas are not confined to the narrow world of arts practitioners and critics. They also soon learn the need to develop new skills in order to relate and explain their work to people, or to work alongside them.

Similarly, there is a need for health care staff to respect the contribution that artists can make, to recognise that their special skills, creativity and imagination can complement their own work with patients. The collaboration of arts therapists and artists is particularly important. Many people outside the health field are confused about the respective roles of the two professions. While there is often overlap in the work, therapists are essentially providing a diagnostic service as part of the clinical team. Artists' work may indeed be therapeutic in the general sense of the word, in that it is helping to heal; but that is only one aim of their work. Happily there are already plenty of examples of artists and arts or occupational therapists working together, where the value of cooperation has been understood. There have even been some places where additional therapists have been employed as a direct result of the impetus given by an arts project. There is clearly

scope for therapists who work with small groups or on a one-to-one basis to play a substantial part in a wide-ranging arts programme. After all, both groups in the end should have the same objective: to work for the benefit of their patients or clients.

The potential for the arts in this sphere is enormous, since everyone needs health care at some point in their lives. Today the arts have become a major activity in the UK in the health care field: around 300 projects provide work for several hundred artists and craftspeople, and access to the arts for thousands of people who would not otherwise have the opportunity to be involved, whether as audience or participants.

This book is an attempt to map out the state of the arts in health care as it stands in 1992. Although there is an increasing amount of imaginative and exciting work going on in many countries, some directly inspired by projects in the UK, such diverse activity would need another book to do it justice. The aim of the present book is to show the rich variety of projects and activities being undertaken in the UK, while highlighting the organisational, social, financial and artistic problems that can arise where innovation and change are taking place. The case-studies are included to provide a detailed, up-to-date picture of four pioneering projects. Although they are best read in the sequence in which they appear in the book, they also stand in their own right and may be read separately from the main text.

The vision, skills and dedication of many individuals have helped to establish a legitimate and valued role for the arts in a variety of health care institutions. The hope now is that what is still only available to a minority of patients in certain areas will, before the end of the millenium, become a basic provision in health care throughout the country.

Chapter 2
Birth of a Movement

'That the arts can be therapeutic is not of course a new idea. But it is an idea whose time has come.'
Sir Richard Attenborough, 1989

In recent years artists and arts groups all over the UK have become involved in working and sharing their skills with people in galleries and museums, prisons, factories and offices, schools and colleges, community centres and arts centres, as well as in hospitals and other health care settings.

Yet 20 years ago the scene was very different; there were still relatively few artists who had both the inclination and the relevant skills to work with and for the public. Despite this, attitudes were beginning to change, as some of the first community arts initiatives began to make their mark, and money began to be available for further projects, residencies and workshops.

This then was the climate in which in 1973 I took the first tentative steps which were to lead to the founding of the Manchester Hospitals' Arts project.* As an artist I had the chance to exhibit some of my paintings in the out-patients' waiting area of Withington Psychiatric Hospital in Manchester. During visits to the exhibition I realised to my surprise and delight that, for some staff and patients, the paintings had helped to transform their environment.

At this time there was, as far as I was aware, very little art of any kind within the Manchester Health Authority. Some of the old hospitals had a few reproductions on the walls; there was the occasional entertainment provided by visiting choirs or bands, usually at Christmas time; and some efforts by staff in children's wards to create a more friendly environment for their young patients. It dawned on me that hospitals were good places for living artists to exhibit their work, and that many would be keen to do so. I also felt that art should be shared with as many people as possible, and that it could have a profound effect on their well-being.

Initially my scheme to set up a project based on this kind of thinking met with little interest. So I offered to begin work as a volunteer in St Mary's Hospital in Manchester. My first overpowering impression of the hospital was one of drabness. There were hardly any paintings or prints on display. Most areas of the

* The first person pronoun used in parts of this chapter refers to Peter Senior.

building - with the exception of the children's and maternity wards - were devoid of colour, apart from the occasional vase of flowers. Fortunately the staff, whose quarters were particularly nondescript and dreary, were ready to welcome anything that would improve the situation.

My idea was to put up a selection of my paintings, and do some murals for the hospital. My priority was to make my services known to as many people as possible, and then to tackle some of the visual disaster areas. But I was as concerned about my relationship with the people who would be affected by these developments as I was about trying to improve the hospital environment. So once or twice a week I walked around the hospital, talking to staff and patients about the paintings, and the kind of improvements they would like to see made to their surroundings.

I started by bringing in some of my own semi-abstract paintings, based mainly on landscape themes of the Derbyshire Peak District, and discussed them with those staff who had expressed interest in having some for their area or department. The breakthrough came with an exhibition of my work in the main out-patients' hall of the Manchester Royal Infirmary, to which St Mary's was linked. I followed this with an exhibition of the staff's art work, which established the area as an exhibition space, and began to show staff the talents of some of their workmates. It also helped to break down departmental barriers and stereotypes: one shop steward, for example, was talked to by people who would not have dreamed of doing so before they had seen his paintings. The exhibiton inspired him to leave his portering job, and to go to art college to take a degree in photography - and later he returned as a member of the arts team.

During these first months it was clear that the support of senior administrators and some of the consultants was vital. I had access to the whole hospital, but did not fit in to the hierarchy. I found that I was accepted everywhere, treated like an equal, and was therefore able to talk with a good cross-section of staff and patients. A badge on my lapel describing me as 'Hospital Artist' proved a valuable passport. Such ease of access is essential for any artist who wants genuinely to involve staff and patients in decisions about their environment.

Since my part-time work was clearly beginning to have an impact, I was eventually able to persuade the Elizabeth Gaskell College where I was teaching to allow me a year's paid secondment to the hospital. In the autumn of 1975 I began work as a full-time hospital artist. The task was a challenging one. Although I had a good-sized office within St Mary's with a desk, a telephone, a filing cabinet, and a supply of stationery, I had no budget or studio space. Only materials used within the hospital were available to me, and I had to work at home at weekends to produce new paintings for the hospital.

From the start I realised it was essential to make contact with the works department, who were responsible for all the decoration in the hospital. It was potentially a delicate relationship, since my ideas might be seen as implied criticism of their work. When I pressed for picture rails for the corridors, for example, they wanted to know who would have to put up the railing and look after the pictures. But they accepted the need for something to brighten up the corridors, and soon became very helpful with labour and materials.

My first major project was to decorate the children's X-ray room, a dark, magnolia-painted place away from the main hospital where young children often had to spend as much as two hours at a time. In consultation with the senior radiographer, who had suggested the idea in order to make the room less frightening, I painted the room to look like a jungle, incorporating light switches, clocks and machinery in the design. Later, murals in the children's ward gave me a chance to involve the children, who designed alphabets which were transferred to the wall. They were then painted with help from the nurses and other staff who had been involved in the staff art exhibition.

This and other early changes to the visual environment were received with enthusiasm by many patients and staff. They also acted as a stimulus for other arts activities, so that gradually it proved possible to introduce poetry, concerts and theatre performances into the hospital departments.

In many cases such visits prompted people within the hospital to take a hobby more seriously, or find expression for it in the hospital. Important to the success of these events was the enthusiasm of a small group of staff, who eventually became the Hospital Arts Club.

The work was beginning to attract local attention, but as yet there were no funds to enable it to continue. However, North West Arts, the regional arts assocation, successfully put my name forward for one of the new Calouste Gulbenkian Foundation 'artists-in-the-community' awards, which would be enough to enable me to continue my work one day a week for two years. I knew that this would not be sufficient to meet the demand. Fortunately it proved possible at this time for four unemployed former art students to be taken on for a year under the Manpower Services Commission's job creation programme. This marked the formation of the first hospital arts team in the country.

The initial reaction to the idea of a team had been cautious. The district administrator was anxious about the kind of art that four long-haired students might produce, and about how approachable they would be. By this time, however, he did trust me sufficiently to support the application. The unions were opposed in principle to the job creation programme, which they felt management could misuse to provide cheap labour and conceal staff cuts. However, they, too, willingly gave their support when they saw that no existing jobs would be replaced.

The artists - three painters and a mural designer - were expected to paint murals in various parts of the hospital, or take on other commissions for sculptures, panels or mobiles, depending on the needs expressed by the different departments. In each case consultation would take place between the arts team, the relevant staff, and the works department. The team might work as a group, or as individuals. Sometimes they worked on site - in the corridor, an out-patients' area, a ward or clinic; at other times they worked on panels in the studio.

A space to work in was obviously an essential requirement for such a team. Happily, once it had

Above *Some of the Manchester arts team and the mural they completed in the out-patients' department of Crumpsall Hospital.* Above right *Members of the second arts team including Peter Senior, far left.*

Below *One of the current arts team, Stuart Webster, working on the stained glass ceiling for the scanner unit at Hope Hospital, featured on the front cover of this book.*

been cleaned out and re-painted, former kitchens provided ample space to accommodate the team in an open-plan studio, with excellent natural roof light and adjoining spaces with sinks, a workshop area, and a small room which we converted into a photographic dark room.

Having a team of full-time artists was one of the key factors in getting recognition and acceptance of the work. The team concept was one I was determined to persist with, because it was clear that working together helped to maintain the creative momentum in such a challenging situation. It was a tricky balancing act, encouraging the team to pursue these commissions while embracing the many approaches and ideas they had to offer. The binding force was the benefit of the work to patients and staff. In retrospect it seems remarkable to me that the arts team worked collectively, when at that time it was unusual for artists to work in a group, especially in front of a highly professional specialist community who had not expected to have an arts team in their midst.

There had been inevitably a major question mark about these young artists' ability to interest and enthuse their audience. Fresh from art college, they were trained to believe in their own skills, their own art, and their own way of doing things. How would they cope with discussing their art with doctors, nurses, cleaners, porters and patients?

There were indeed some difficulties at first, as Peter Coles found when he visited the project in those early days:

'The arts team and their work were constantly watched and talked about; there were grumbles, snide comments, alarmed apprehension, and even fears of total anarchy, leading to the collapse of the national health service and society in general.

The presence of Peter Senior and four young artists in a hospital was bound to provoke some sort of reaction; it would have been a sad indictment if there had been none. But the criticism just reflected conservative inertia, with no one at this stage trying to stop them.' (1)

Despite these initial problems, the artists were in general accepted by the hospital community as new members of staff, and as individuals with particular styles, techniques, and opinions about art. However, some did find it hard to make contact with hospital staff, feeling that this was outside their job description as artists. Some tended to work mostly on their personal paintings, and so never quite became part of the team. Accustomed from art school to concentrate on their own development, the team found it strange to have a responsibility towards lots of different people, many of whom 'knew nothing about art'. Some members also became annoyed or disheartened at criticisms of their work.

Another difficulty was our relations with the Occupational Therapy Department. From the beginning I had steered away from any therapeutic label for the arts in hospitals. Partly this was to avoid encroaching on the work of the occupational therapists. But I also wanted to avoid our work being seen as art therapy with patients - not least because, if anything, we were practising occupational therapy with the staff.

In 1977, funding for the team came to an unexpected halt. But by now the artists had begun to be accepted, and there were protests from hospital staff and patients at their imminent disappearance. Happily, the job creation programme eventually agreed to fund a new team for the whole of 1978.

The second team of six, which included two artists from the first team, had the advantage of not being pioneers. But they also tended to be less introverted than the first team, and more confident about making contact with the wider hospital world. They were soon busy working on murals, graphics, hanging paintings, organising exhibitions, encouraging photographic work in our dark room, and generally getting to know staff in all departments. We also often had volunteers and students from Manchester Polytechnic (now Manchester Metropolitan University) and elsewhere working with the team, as well as two part-time artists funded by the local authority's community education programme.

In addition to the visual arts activities, we began to build up a strong performance programme. This involved both professional performers - musicians, poets, dancers, puppeteers, actors and writers - and the arts team members, who soon developed new skills in these areas, and began to work skilfully with patients. This was an important step: I believe strongly that everyone is creative, and that it's just a question of finding the appropriate means and techniques that will suit their different personalities, and enable them to express their creativity.

During that first phase of the project I had no idea how it would turn out, or even if people would tolerate someone going round saying they should have more arts activities. For me the amazing thing was that people responded positively, instead of just putting up with the the project passively.

When the job creation programme money finally ran out, the project went through a difficult two years, living from month to month on donations while we looked for alternative long-term funding. During this difficult time it was impossible to plan ahead, and many ideas and large-scale projects had to be shelved. Finally, in 1980 we were awarded a grant for three years from the Manchester and Salford Inner Cities Urban Aid Partnership, on the condition that we concentrate more on hospitals, health centres and clinics in the whole Manchester Health Authority inner-city area. This gave the work a much-needed stability, as did the subsequent money from the Department of the Environment's Inner Cities Initiative. The arts team was able to expand to ten, many of whom are still involved with the project. (See page 16 for an account of the project's current work.)

Ideas and initiatives seldom develop in isolation. By this time a number of projects were being developed in other hospitals, and we began to see our work in Manchester as part of a wider movement in the field of health care. In 1976, about the time our first arts team started, the dancer Gina Levete had founded the agency SHAPE. Her aim was to bring professional artists into contact with groups who were isolated from the rest of the community - including elderly and mentally ill people, and people in hospitals, day centres and residential homes. Although her work was very different from ours, there were obvious similarities - not least in SHAPE's emphasis on the value of communication, and the healing potential of the arts.

But it was only in 1981, at a conference I organised in Manchester, that I first became aware of how many projects there were in the field, and how much interest the idea was generating. The enthusiasm was stimulating, the quality of the discussions high. Delegates, who came from all over the UK as well as overseas, became aware of the contributions being made by different forms of art, from murals and puppetry to music and mime. Many recommendations were made, including one that information on the role of the arts and artists in health care should be collated, so that pressure could be put on government departments to increase awareness and highlight the value of the work. Another recommendation was that there should be a significant percentage within the budgets for all new hospitals, health centres and other such buildings to provide facilities for the arts - an idea that has since been widely discussed, though it has yet to become government policy as it has in some states in the USA and in several European countries.

In fact, it was not long before a response came from a government department. Following a seminar on Art in Hospitals at the Institute of Contemporary Arts in London in 1982, Howard Goodman, who was then Director of Development at the Department of Health and Social Security, invited a small group of us involved in the work to meet to discuss the potential for his department's involvement. One of the first fruits of this was the commissioning in 1983 of a feasibility study into the potential for the arts within the whole of the Isle of Wight Health Authority. Written by Peter Coles, it had a major impact on the strategy which was subsequently adopted by the authority, where plans had been agreed the previous year for an exciting new project: the building of a new St Mary's Hospital in Newport. (2)

Not only was this to be the first low-energy hospital in the country, but the first in which consideration would be given at the planning stage as to how the arts could be incorporated into the overall design plan. In 1984 I was invited by Howard Goodman to collaborate with the architect Richard Burton, and became arts adviser to the project. Until this time most arts in health care work had been within existing, often old, hospital buildings. So this was an important landmark in the fight to gain recognition of the need for the arts in new hospitals, health centres and other such buildings. It also provided an excellent opportunity for us to explore the professional relationship between architect and artist. (For a fuller account of the Isle of Wight initiative see page 84.)

It was during this period, 1982-1984, that the Attenborough Committee of Inquiry into the Arts and Disabled People, of which I was a member, carried out its work. It was clear to the committee that the arts in health care was one of the largest areas of activity to be considered - it was estimated that some 60 hospitals were using the services of artists, designers and craftsmen. It concluded that within hospitals the untapped potential for arts development remained vast. While identifying many examples of good practice, including the Manchester Hospitals' Arts project, it also pinpointed some of the difficulties, and highlighted the importance for arts activities and projects to evolve from within, rather than be imposed from outside.

The resulting Attenborough Report, *Arts and Disabled People*, was hard-hitting. It said that 'the present arrangements for using the arts in the NHS are far too haphazard to enable their full potential to be realised'. It recommended that the government require regional and district health authorities to develop the use of the arts, and establish programmes for using the services of artists. It also said that district health authorities should each designate an officer to be responsible for coordinating the provision of arts opportunities and developing arts programmes. Finally, it recommended that the brief for any new hospital or redevelopment should include the provision of works of art and of facilities for arts activities. (3)

The report was influential, and helped to encourage government ministers, civil servants, health authorities, administrators and managers to give more attention to developing a better quality of life for patients, and a better working environment for staff within all health buildings. Arts projects and residencies began to proliferate, and to be extended into hospices and health centres. Meanwhile, funding and enabling bodies such as the regional arts

associations, the Artists' Agency, the Public Art Development Trust, and others began to give the work more attention. In 1986 the Department of Health and Social Security acknowledged the importance of the arts in health care:

'Works of art enhance the interiors of health buildings; their provision should be incorporated into the architect's brief and the project budget. The employment of artists in various media has not only furthered this objective, but has successfully involved patients, staff and volunteers in environmental improvements.' (4)

However, progress was still patchy, and in some areas of the country virtually non-existent. Working as a member of the Carnegie Council, a watchdog body set up to review and monitor the effect of the Attenborough Report, I was asked to review arts developments in the health field. The council's report, *After Attenborough*, published in 1988, reflected both the successes and disappointments. The chapter devoted to 'The Arts and Health' concluded:

'We wish to affirm strongly that the arts activity which has developed within the health sector in recent years is of a most creative nature. Many who are sick or disabled have chosen to join with able-bodied people in a common enjoyment of the arts, and this in turn is having a humanising effect on their physical and social environment. These activities are, however, small-scale and spasmodic, in relation to the needs of patients in health care settings. We trust that health service administrators at every level will recognise the purpose and benefits of the arts as an integral feature of improvements in health care generally.' (5)

Around this time there was a growing feeling that the time had come for the establishment of a national organisation or centre, to give guidance on the use of the arts to health authorities, health managers and others wishing to develop an arts initiative in the health care field. As a consequence Arts for Health was established in May 1988 at Manchester Polytechnic, and I became the director. Our aim was to provide information, advice and a consultancy service, and to give practical help to arts projects of all kinds in relation to funding, planning, management, monitoring and evaluation. We also wanted to establish a network to assist and link all those involved in the field.

In the five years since the setting up of Arts for Health, there has been a substantial increase in the number of arts projects in the health care field in the UK. In 1983, 65 British hospitals were putting some of their own money into arts provision; by 1992 it was possible to identify at least 300 projects around the country, with new ones starting up all the time. The rest of this book looks in detail at some of the major artistic and organisational issues that have arisen during the development of such projects. It draws on the experiences of a considerable number of people who have pioneered this valuable and rewarding work, and who have generously shared their ideas and experiences in order to make the book as comprehensive and as useful as possible.

Hospices are giving encouragement to arts activities: this book was compiled by Chrissie Gittins from words of patients, relatives and staff while she was writer-in-residence at Springhill Hospice, Rochdale, 1990/91.

A Matter of Teamwork

Hospital Arts, Manchester

'Hospitals need the balance of elements such as wholeness, happiness, health, fun. So the members of the team concentrate on these, because we see them as essential.'

Christine Bull has been in a good position to back up this philosophy with practical action. As manager of Hospital Arts since 1979, she has been involved, together with the other nine members of her team, in a wide range of artistic projects. Their work has not only brought dramatic improvements to the visual environment of many hospitals and health centres in Manchester over the years, but has enabled hundreds of patients and many staff to find new purpose by being involved in artistic activities, as well as provided enjoyment for huge numbers of visitors.

Hospital Arts has come a long way since its inception in the mid-1970s. Today the team members not only work as artists and performers within particular health care settings, but also act as consultants, animateurs and trainers - sometimes well beyond the confines of Manchester. The team has also spawned two independent projects, the Reminiscence Project and the START arts centre and studio. (The two projects are described on pages 66 and 44 respectively.)

Care means 'looking after feelings as well as bodies': a performance event by Manchester Hospital Arts.

The Hospital Arts team believes health care should be a question of looking after feelings as well as bodies. Artist Brian Chapman, the team's artistic coordinator, says they aim to establish a balance. 'Institutions such as hospitals can seem very cold, clinical and calculating,' he says. 'The arts can add a new dimension. We aim to look at places through the eyes of the people who use them.'

Putting the patient first means making sure that individual projects are geared to what people need or want. This means careful consultation with nursing and other staff at each stage. Projects can vary enormously, and may involve painting, photography, murals, mosaic, stained glass, drama, reminiscence, or a wide mix of musical performances and workshops. At times the brief may be clear-cut and well-defined, at others more open-ended and unpredictable, patients and staff defining the direction of what takes place.

A good example of the latter kind of project is Hospital Arts' recent collaboration with the North Manchester Community Mental Health Team. Musicians Sarah McKernan and Pete Hughes offered musical activity sessions to clients on a drop-in basis in a community centre in Crumpsall. The content had been thrashed out with the health workers, and was based on the participants' musical interests. The result was a stimulating mix of different types of music - big band, pop, songs from shows, with Valentine's Day and St Patrick's Day providing a focus for love songs and Irish music.

The Hospital Arts team led the sessions, not as performers but as catalysts, encouraging the patients to take part in their own way in what was essentially a shared experience. Over the eight sessions a strong group feeling was built up, prompting participants to come up with their own ideas. One woman recited some of her poetry; another, who loved dancing, demonstrated steps and sequences.

The project was judged a success, not least because most people who attended didn't miss a session. 'This kind of activity breaks down roles, it gives participants a sense of sharing or initiating activity,' Sarah McKernan recalls. 'They gained confidence in talking in an atmosphere where their contribution was invited and

Reassuring but dignified: the Nightingale Centre at Withington Hospital, Manchester.

valued.' Mary Bass, of the community team, was equally pleased with the results: 'Hospital Arts were welcoming and non-threatening from the start, they didn't set themselves apart as performers,' she remembers. 'Sarah and Pete displayed warmth, respect and understanding in sometimes difficult circumstances. Some individuals who are usually quite shy visibly gained confidence through participation. It was a very positive thing to see people we would never have imagined doing so getting up and singing.'

Participation is also one of the main aims of the team's current project at Ashworth Special Hospital in Merseyside. Backed by a year's Home Office funding, Brian Chapman, Anna Todd and Stuart Webster are working there with patients in a medium dependency male ward. The medical staff and management set up the scheme with Hospital Arts in an attempt to provide the patients with more positive and interesting surroundings. They are now being drawn in to make decisions and choices about their environment, and to taking part in doing the work, applying decorative paint effects and creating artwork, as well as selecting furnishings and fittings.

After eight weeks on the project, Brian Chapman is delighted with progress. 'The fact that the patients are mentally ill and have committed a crime means it's a different context from working in a mental health unit,' he says. 'So at first I was apprehensive, I had the idea it would be heavy and dangerous. But it's gelled somehow, I think because of the fun element we've put into it.' He feels the work is beginning to achieve its object of changing the nature of the regime which the patients experience. 'There were arts activities before, but the patients tended to be sent off to do things: they were told what to do and how to do it. Our aim is to give them a sense of ownership, and to have an effect on the social atmosphere. We want the collaborative working to encourage trust and respect, to raise morale, and be an opportunity to have some fun.'

Improvements to any group of patients' visual surroundings clearly need to be carefully matched to their emotional needs. Hospital Arts' work at the Nightingale Centre in Withington Hospital, Manchester shows how this can be achieved. The centre, a breast-screening facility for women from the north west, is housed in a renovated workhouse chapel. In the planning discussions between the architects, health workers and Hospital Arts, it was agreed that priority should be given to creating an atmosphere that would ease the anxieties of the women patients.

Hospital Arts' solution was a series of panels for the reception area, suggesting plants, water and landscape. Soft green and blue pastel colours and delicate, flowing lines characterise the panels, which are arch-shaped to echo the former chapel's tall, narrow stained glass windows. 'It's a good example of creating a reassuring but dignified atmosphere,' Sarah McKernan says. Staff in the centre have also reacted positively to the gentle tranquillity of the artwork. The centre's receptionist says: 'The atmosphere in here has a physical effect: it's so restful, it helps the staff deal calmly with the people who come in for tests.'

Themes for projects undertaken by Hospital Arts are often suggested by individual health workers. On the children's surgical ward at St Mary's Hospital in Manchester, for example, staff were worried about the number of children involved in road accidents, and asked Hospital Arts to turn the ward corridor into a street. As you walk down it, you pass a miniature belisha beacon, a pelican crossing and traffic lights, all in working order. On one side is a miniature phone box, in which children can play at reporting accidents. On the wall are cut-outs of children following or breaking the Green Cross Code, with large ticks or crosses against the right and wrong kind of behaviour. Children are encouraged to contribute their own work to the scene, for example on painted brick walls left blank for their painted cats or dogs to be added. 'It gives them a purposeful space to play with,' Brian Chapman says.

This project also benefited from collaboration between the artists and other groups. Students from Manchester Polytechnic did the cut-outs; the police advised on road-safety aspects; the medical engineers in the hospital made the miniature traffic lights; and British Telecom installed the phone box. In addition, during the two weeks when the ward was being redecorated, the artists worked with the decorators masking out certain sections of the upper walls to get the cloud and brick-wall effects.

Streetwise: road safety is the name of the game in the children's surgical ward, St Mary's Hospital, Manchester.

Sometimes the Hospital Arts team work directly with children, both in hospitals and outside. For a project designed to give a new look to the entrance to Shaw Heath

The new look for the Shaw Heath Health Centre, Stockport, created by primary school children.

Health Centre in Stockport, some 40 older children were recruited from Cale Green Primary School. Their task was to create a large and colourful mural, to cheer up the stark and forbidding brick walls in the clinic's entrance.

Working with the artist in their school, each child painted an image of a house on to a panel. The group's work was then assembled into an 18-foot townscape for display in the clinic's entrance. Apart from its impact on patients, the vibrant and detailed artwork greatly benefited the children, according to headteacher Barbara Mallon: 'The children were given a lot of encouragement by Hospital Arts, and the project enhanced the artwork in the rest of the school,' she says. 'I think it's very important that the children play a part in the community, so that they value it as they grow up.'

In many projects the process of making is as important as the finished result. Elderly patients at a day hospital in Salford took an active part in a scheme to transform their bare and functional bathroom into something altogether different. Encouraged by Brian Chapman, they chose an oriental theme and helped decide on designs. Wood panels stencilled with translucent lacquer show the four seasons

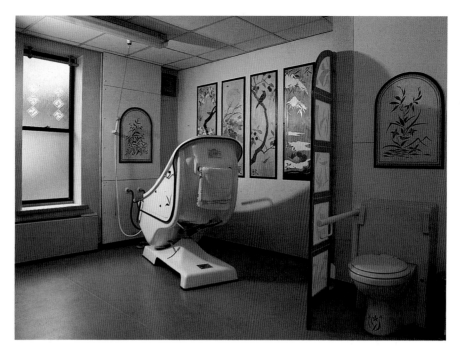

in Japanese style, leaf and bamboo shapes make a design motif for ceiling tiles, sand-blasted perspex mobiles and a folding screen. Brian Chapman adapted techniques to people's physical abilities, making it easier for them to join in and ensuring an effective result.

The quality of the finished work raised everyone's confidence and inspired them to do more. Staff saw their patients achieve more than they would have thought possible, and the older people were enthusiastic. 'I've never done anything like this before; it was so interesting and so professional,' one of the patients said. 'In fact I've enjoyed it so much I don't want it to end.'

The Hospital Arts team - consisting of musicians, artists, and a photographer - undertake these and many other projects from a former chest clinic off Oxford Road in Manchester, which is in useful proximity to both the Royal Infirmary and St Mary's Hospitals. The premises include a studio, a large storage room, a design room, smaller rooms for the individual artists, and a dark room.

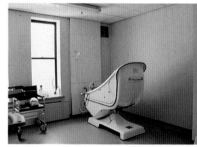

The team is now a relatively stable one, but the climate in which they work is markedly different from what it was even five years ago. 'The biggest change is that we've been put into the market place,' Brian Chapman explains. 'The NHS quality initiative has made things different, with those committees set up to look into the quality of life wanting to work with us. We're planning in a less ad hoc way now, sometimes as much as four or five years ahead. We've also had to be more professional in how we present proposals to clients, in having proper contracts, and so on.'

Finance is always likely to be a problem. During the 1980s there was substantial support from the Inner Cities Initiative, amounting to £72,000 in 1987, its final year. Nowadays, apart from what the team earns in fees and commissions, the main support comes from the three District Health Authorities of Central, North and South Manchester - Manchester City Council ended their support in 1991. This funding is significant, in that it gives formal acknowledgement to the idea that the arts are an integral part of health care. Funding from North West Arts also allows Hospital Arts' services to be offered to clients at a reasonable fee.

Elderly patients in Salford Hospital played an active part in transforming their bathroom. Middle and top *Before and after the project.* Above *Team member Brian Chapman working with patients.*

'The future lies in saying that money for the arts should come from health budgets,' says Christine Bull. 'If you believe that what you're doing is beneficial, then you can say that.' But she also stresses that the tighter time constraints can cause problems for the team. 'It's not always easy to know how long a project will take, to account for the time needed for failure or experiment, for the fact that you don't always have a brilliant idea on day one. Everything we do is a one-off created for a different place and the people there.'

Such pressures would not suit every artist nor, she suggests, every temperament. 'People who are very shy and inhibited won't cope: you need an ability to get on with people.' Brian Chapman agrees, and adds: 'You need to be open, responsive and patient, a good problem-solver, able to work to deadlines, and the kind of person who finds it equally easy to talk to the chief executive and the cleaner.'

Developing and maintaining good relations with nursing staff and others who work closely with patients is seen as a key part of the artists' work. The team find that many staff feel oppressed by the bureaucracy of the system, and greatly welcome new ideas. 'It's difficult for them to break through the "This is how we've always done it" attitude,' Sarah McKernan says. 'But if you go in and work with them, it stimulates and gives support to their ideas. It can be hard for them to initiate new activity and keep going in a place day after day. We provide a framework to break through this barrier.'

Like other artists, the Hospital Arts team have needed to ensure that their work doesn't encroach on that of the arts and occupational therapists. In practice, although the projects may prove to be therapeutic, the artists are not working in the diagnostic way that therapists do. 'We may be professional artists, but we're not challenging those other professionals,' Christine Bull says. 'It's no business of ours to know what's wrong with someone, unless there's a safety element.' Projects of course often do prove therapeutic; several have shown that it's possible for the two professions to establish a modus vivendi, and work fruitfully together.

Outsiders sometimes ask why it's necessary to have a team of salaried artists, why the projects can't be commissioned on an individual basis. Although this has

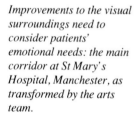

Improvements to the visual surroundings need to consider patients' emotional needs: the main corridor at St Mary's Hospital, Manchester, as transformed by the arts team.

happened occasionally, Hospital Arts believes that continuity, collaborative working and a broad base of skills offer substantial advantages, both to the artists and their clients. 'You're dealing with stressful work, which needs a support system,' Brian Chapman says. 'So you need people who have been in it for a number of years, who understand the issues. Being part of a team also encourages change: we learn from each other, we use each others' skills to be more innovative. If we were working in isolation, it would be very different. This way we have more to offer our clients.'

As the largest and longest-established health care arts team in the country, Hospital Arts inevitably continues to attract a great deal of outside interest, especially from health managers and arts administrators hoping to go down the same path. Meanwhile, on their home ground the team's work continues to receive widespread praise, both for the quality of their art and performance work, and the skill with which they involve both patients and staff.

'Critics are few and far between,' Christine Bull says. 'Most people welcome what we are doing. They may not understand it, but they like it because it produces a change for the better, it's not something imposed from outside, and it involves people at all levels working together.'

Entertaining children with 'Gurgley's Dicky Ticker', a clowning show which toured the wards of Manchester hospitals.

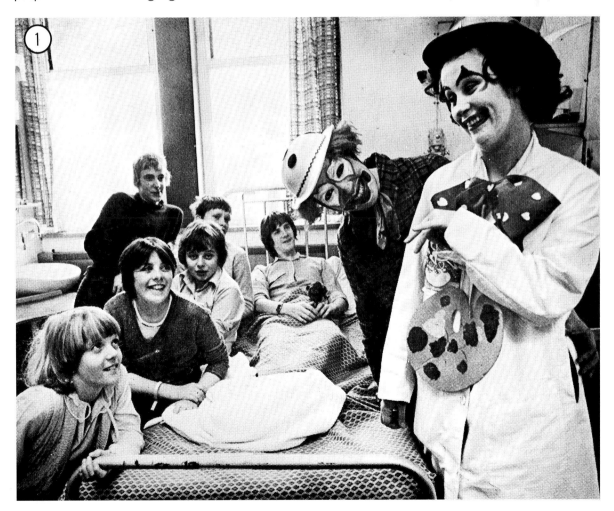

Chapter 3
The Visual Environment

'What Italy could afford in the Middle Ages, we could afford now, if we had a true sense of values: they would not have jibbed at engaging Giotto to paint the walls of a hospital for lepers.'
John Davis, 1989

It's hard to think of anything more depressing to patients, staff and visitors than the empty, dreary corridors that unfortunately still characterise so many of today's hospitals. All too often, in many of the older buildings, the effect of an inappropriate design is made much worse by the poor condition of the building. In 1989 I visited the West Middlesex Hospital in Isleworth*. Originally built as a workhouse in the nineteenth century, it now occupies a site packed with ugly buildings of every shape and size. With me was Sir Richard Attenborough, who later recalled the beginning of our visit:

'We were taken along a vast, echoing corridor, well over 100 yards long. Although the walls had received a coat of gloss paint quite recently, I was horrified to see whole areas that looked like something out of a horror film, the paint - under the onslaught of incurable rising damp - literally falling off, and plaster beneath erupting into monstrous carbuncles oozing slimy mould. As we walked along we wondered how anyone could hope to get well or remain cheerful in such an environment of decay. Then we came to a staircase next to wards where young children and adolescents were recovering from psychiatric illness. And here, suddenly, the whole atmosphere of the place changed, because two young artists had been at work, painting the walls

*The first person pronoun used in parts of this chapter refers to Peter Senior.

with vigorous vegetation - creepers, leaves, butterflies and birds. In no sense was it "fine art", but it was the finest possible sight in that particular hospital, a testament to the optimistic power of the human spirit, and a powerful reminder of how the simplest scheme can have an enormous psychological effect.' (1)

The empty spaces

Sadly, it is not only the older hospital buildings that provide such a depressing experience. Even some of our newer buildings have interminable corridors - a recent survey showed that doctors had to walk up to 16 miles a day during their shifts. (2) Howard Goodman, for many years the chief architect and director of health buildings for the Department of Health and Social Security, has suggested that this may be because 'corridors belong to no one or to no one department, and only offer rights of passage'. (3) Whatever the cause, it is hardly surprising that where artists or arts teams have been brought into hospitals, one of their priorities has invariably been to 'do something to brighten up the corridors'.

The project undertaken by the Manchester Hospitals' Arts team at Withington Hospital is a typical example of the kind of challenge faced by artists in such circumstances. The hospital's vast, rambling complex had been developed around the old Chorlton workhouse, the centrepiece of which was

One panel from the 80-foot mural by Faye Carey, originally in St Stephen's Hospital, Fulham, relocated in the new Chelsea and Westminster Hospital.

The main corridor at Withington Hospital, Manchester, before and after treatment by the arts team.

believed to be the longest hospital corridor in Europe, stretching out for about a quarter of a mile. It was suffering from damp and deteriorating plasterwork, had a strong chequerboard linoleum covering, and was painted throughout in cream, grey and pea-green. The central dishwashing area was on the corridor, which meant it was often cluttered with trucks, or carrying pots waiting to be washed up. Leading off it were the psychiatric hospital, the maternity hospital and many wards.

Our first step was to make sure that the estates department could make good the plasterwork and carry out the necessary general repairs before we started. The next was to find out from staff what function each of the areas performed. We then presented to the management a design comprising seven themes, relating to these functions. We suggested having murals or large panels which made use of spaces between windows, or of the natural 'picture frame' arches which occurred down the length of the corridor. The themes chosen included the English country garden, the local environment, tropical landscapes, Greek myths and legends, and the elements. The work also produced portraits of the pathology technician and the head cleaner, a puppet booth near the children's ward, and a series of spectacular murals around the dark lift areas.

Apart from transforming the corridor beyond recognition, the project had other consequences. We were able to draw the management's attention to a fine but deteriorating glazed verandah, which could be seen through one of the corridor windows. Instead of it then being knocked down as planned, it was restored and renovated, and is now a beautiful feature. The dishwashing area was eventually relocated, and its place taken by a snack bar and shop. The arts team were consulted on its design, and helped with the facade, blending it in with existing themes. Although redecoration has taken place since the scheme was implemented, the works department consulted with the arts team so that the new decoration would complement the murals.

Contact and consultation

The two artists who did most of the work on the Withington project were given a suite of redundant offices on the corridor for use as studios. This meant that staff were able to drop in and observe progress on the panels being painted there, or see the murals develop as they were painted directly onto the corridor walls. Experience has shown that this kind of continuing contact between artists and hospital staff during the life of such projects, as well as a thorough initial consultation, can be vital to their success. Several projects have nearly foundered because staff, whether an individual or a group, have not been sufficiently informed about or aware of its content and purpose, or when plans have been changed without due consultation.

One somewhat comic example of the latter occurred recently at the Royal Berkshire Hospital in Reading, where the main entrance and corridor were to be redesigned and redecorated. An artist who had been selected to paint a mural outside the children's ward withdrew at the last minute, and a replacement was found at short notice. Christopher Barrett, the artist in charge of the project, recalls what happened next: 'The artist went full speed ahead with his theme of animals with humans playing musical instruments. Then one night at ten o'clock he was rung up and instructed not to come in again until a conference about the mural could be arranged. It seems that a team of psychiatrists happened to be passing, and felt the work to be totally unsuitable - "because there were too many phallic symbols in it". In fact the real problem was nothing to do with flutes and rhino horns, but a pictorial one: the scale was too large and the tonal contrast too violent. But people can only feel confident to express their unease using their own area of expertise. However, the effect of the incident on the artist was pretty devastating.' (4)

A more serious example of incomplete consultation arose during the arts project started at the Devonshire Royal Hospital in Buxton, a remarkable circular building with what was once the largest dome in Europe, originally built as an equestrian centre, and now an orthopaedic and rehabilitation hospital. The wards are situated around the circumference, leaving a vast, under-used, echoing and intimidating central space. In 1990 Arts for Health helped to initiate an arts project there. Part of the project involved patients and staff creating small panels of mosaic for a new, 20-foot high mosaic column in the middle of the large central domed space. After the structure had been built, but before the mosaics had been done, one doctor and other staff expressed the view that the column was not appropriate to the architecture of the building or the patient care, and said he wanted it stopped. At the subsequent crisis meeting, at which the artist and nurse coordinating the project explained the concept, and the support for the solution by patients, it transpired that the doctors had not been adequately informed about the project. All staff had been invited to the presentation to

launch the mosaic project - it was decided *not* to target medical staff specifically. The crisis was averted, working arrangements for the rest of the projects were quickly formalised, and a committee set up to ensure information went out regularly to everyone from then on.

Ironically, the Buxton 'Spa Arts' project, as it was soon called, was and still is in many ways a model for consultation and patient involvement and has been adopted by Stockport Area Health Authority in setting up an arts coordinator post and a new project.

The mosaic column (and 'teapot' detail, overleaf) at the Devonshire Royal Hospital in Buxton, Derbyshire, filling an under-used and intimidating space.

An enthusiastic theatre sister, Sylvia Fradley, organised the presentation for staff, patients and the community by Arts for Health. Subsequently an arts committee was formed and it was agreed to set up a multi-disciplinary project to improve the physical and social environment of the hospital. The hospital and health authority management agreed to Alison Creed, a part-time nurse with a committed interest in the arts, taking on the responsibility of coordinating the arts project and liaising with all concerned. Alison devised

and distributed a questionnaire to staff and patients, out of which emerged the idea of the mosaic centre-piece, and the choice of the theme of water. Langley Brown, local artist and director of START studios (see page 44), organised the collaboration between the studios and Spa Arts, together with Alison Creed. He then brainstormed with patients and staff in the wards for visual ideas, asking people to come up with instant sketches of what was in their mind. From these sessions the ideas for the final mosaic design emerged. The creation of the panels involved an

The Noah's Ark play sculpture designed and made by George Carter for a Children's Play Courtyard designed by Sarah Hosking.

impressive number of participants: 64 patients, 27 members of staff, and 42 people from the community.

Not all projects have such happy endings. In one southern hospital, a children's play courtyard with a huge mural and a Noah's Ark was closed the day after it was officially opened, despite being cleared for safety by the local authority inspector. The arts coordinator involved, Sarah Hosking, said: 'The district manager left and the unit manager left and it's been closed for three years. If your top man changes, you've got problems. They say it's too sunny for the children and there's a risk of legionnaire's disease from the fountain. The staff say they wanted a Wendy House. It cost £36,000 and the health authority didn't pay a penny. Sometimes I don't think hospitals deserve art.' (5)

The Devonshire Royal Hospital example also shows how a project that begins with the aim of improving the environment can end up having other positive results, and develop in different directions. Staff soon began to realise the beneficial social effects of patients working alongside nurses and ambulance drivers in a shared art activity, and once the mosaic was completed a permanent weekly art class was set up in the dome area. The arts programme has expanded, and the hospital has hosted several arts

events, including circus workshops, brass-band concerts, dance performances, and textile making. Meanwhile, in an attempt to give the community the feeling that the hospital is theirs, community groups are being offered the chance to use this unique arts space. One already doing so is Connect 90, an arts group bringing together able-bodied and disabled people, which has started a photography project with START. The group is given space on condition that hospital patients are also involved. Connect 90, supported by Buxton and Blackbrook Community Education Council, was also actively involved in Spa Arts - especially 'Buxton by the Sea', a large community textile, by Adrienne Brown.

Many of the newer projects are making sure that community involvement is substantial. At the new Mid Sussex Hospital in Hayward's Heath, the arts project is making use of a wide variety of media - paintings, sculpture, tapestries, patchwork, ceramic murals, batik. Students from Brighton Polytechnic (now the University of Brighton) are making mobiles to decorate the children's ward; community college students are also being involved; wallhangings are being produced and donated by local embroiderers' and quilters' guilds; and most of the surrounding parish councils are giving a picture of their village to the wards' day rooms, each of which is named after one of them. Such collaboration helps to break down the isolation in which many of the older hospitals still operate. (6)

Paintings on the walls

Many hospital arts projects have started with a scheme to purchase or commission paintings or drawings to hang on the walls, in order to provide decoration, and brighten up the general appearance of the building. The largest art collection of this kind is in St Thomas's Hospital in London, where there are some 600 works by 200 artists, from Victor Pasmore to Richard Smith, and including recent work by young graduates. A part-time art curator maintains and catalogues the collection, which appears to be liked by both staff and the general public. The selection of pictures to be bought is made by a high-powered committee involving, among others, an architect, a consultant and the dean. (7)

The art gallery at Aberdeen Royal Infirmary.

One of the most impressive displays of original art works in any hospital is to be found at the Aberdeen Royal Infirmary, which is the centre for the Grampian Hospitals Art Project. Significantly, the project was initiated by a consultant at the hospital, Norman Matheson, and colleagues. By donation, purchase and commission, a valuable collection of contemporary Scottish visual art has been built up, and now numbers more than 500 works.

Some of the panels of the 'Waterfalls' mural by Melvyn Chantry in the Chelsea and Westminster Hospital, London.

More modest schemes are generally run either by a hospital's League of Friends, or by an art committee. In both cases they may not fully represent the interests and wishes of patients or staff. Such schemes immediately raise issues about control and consultation. A recent example of this was at Leicester Royal Infirmary, which has a collection administered in a similar way to that of St Thomas's. An art committee has been in existence for many years and has put together a remarkably fine collection of paintings, prints, and drawings. Sadly, the project has remained the province of a small group of people, with staff knowing very little about it. There is little appreciation of the works on display, because few people know anything about them, or their origins. There is also a feeling amongst staff that patients should have been involved in some way.

Selection of artworks is always going to be a tricky matter, especially where work from staff and volunteers is having to be considered. Mary Potter, from the Princess Royal Hospital Arts Project in Lewes, Sussex, reflects the experience of several arts coordinators and artists when she says: 'Subject matter and artistic standards are a problem: staff on the whole tend to want poor-quality, popular-style art.' (8) Julie de Bastion, one of the artists involved with the new Cannock Community Hospital in Staffordshire, encountered a similar response: 'When I first submitted my drawings and preliminary pastel sketches, the leaning amongst the two dozen staff vetting the work was towards the mediocre and the banal. They preferred the safe and compromising, as opposed to the creative and personal.' (9)

"NURSE, CAN YOU FIND ME A BED NEAR A LESS POPULAR PICTURE".

Clearly a firm policy is needed to avoid this kind of occurrence. At the Queen's Medical Centre in Nottingham, which has a large children's department, the hospital had been deluged with work from enthusiastic volunteers and nursery nurses. The paediatric nursing officer, Elizabeth Fradd, had come to realise that it was necessary to have a careful policy about the range, quality and amount of work to be put up by staff in the many wards and corridors. Today these areas are benefiting from having work which has been carefully chosen to be part of an overall scheme, and includes commissions from outside professional artists.

Public commissions

The Leicester Royal Infirmary programme also included the commissioning of artists and sculptors to create works for specific sites. Many hospitals, especially during the 1980s when art in public places bloomed, have chosen this as a way of improving the landscape, creating interest in an entrance, or providing a focus in a neglected area. With the support of their regional arts board, and with other professional advice, hospitals have engaged the talents of some top professional artists to create large-scale works. Among the best-known are Michael Kenny's wall-mounted sculpture at Addenbrooke's Hospital in Cambridge and Peter Randall-Page's Portland stone sculpture in one of the main courtyards of the Leicester Royal Infirmary. Very recently commissions have been given to Patrick Heron and Allen Jones for major works for the new Chelsea and Westminster Hospital.

Since responses to art are so personal and subjective, it is inevitable that some public commissions have provoked controversy, both within and outside the hospital. At Glenfield Hospital in Nottingham, for example, a piece of sculpture by Sokari Douglas Camp, chosen by an art committee, was variously labelled 'the tin men' or 'the white bra' by hospital staff, and was generally the subject of ridicule - although some did say it had a certain curious charm, or that it provided a talking point. Another sculpture that caused controversy was one purchased from Bill

Right *Maquette and the final version of the 'Acrobatic Dancer' by Allen Jones, a 60-foot steel sculpture for the Chelsea and Westminster Hospital, London.*

Pye for the Sheffield Children's Hospital. Placed outside the front entrance, it was referred to locally as the 'stainless steel knot', and was thought by many people to be quite inappropriate for a children's hospital. Eventually it was moved to another less prominent position on the same site.

The needs of patients

Any unusual piece of art is going to excite controversy - that is part of what art is about - and no amount of prior consultation is going to cater for everyone's taste. These examples and others like them do, however, underline the need for as much information and explanation as possible to be given when works of art are being positioned in public places. In the case of hospitals and other health care institutions, of course, there are additional factors to be considered. Depending on where the work is to be positioned, special care and thought needs to be given to the feelings and medical condition of those likely to see it. Here, content, choice of colour, materials, shape and line can be very important.

A good example of a successful commission was Graham Crowley's 'Birds', a series of colourful enamelled cut-outs created for the walls and pillars of the out-patients department at Brompton Hospital in London. Patients with chest complaints said that the spaciousness and free-floating nature of the design helped their breathing problems. Having initially been given the chance to choose from different designs by four artists, they chose the 'Birds' design because it was felt to be 'colourful,

cheerful and reassuringly restful'. (10) But restfulness is not necessarily everyone's priority in these circumstances. Artist Beverley Fry, who did a vivid painting for the main entrance to the new Cannock Community Hospital in Staffordshire, says: 'I've been told the vibrance of the colour is very uplifting, and the light luminosity that you can achieve in water colour gives a happy, light feeling.' (11)

Artists clearly need to be especially sensitive to the needs of patients when potentially disturbing images are being used. A forthcoming report *Evaluating Art in Hospitals*, based on research in Oxford hospitals, suggests that artists should avoid creating angry surrealist paintings or abstract works that might remind patients of internal organs or blood slides. It records how a mural entitled 'Liner' in the Radcliffe Infirmary was criticised by staff and patients, because it included rats in the composition: this was considered upsetting for patients who might be waiting for enemas and already be feeling nauseous. The report's authors also suggest that shapes reminiscent of anatomy and expressions of pain are best avoided, as well as too much blood-red or black. (12)

The experience at the Radcliffe underlines the importance of a carefully worked out, sensitive and precise commissioning policy for any public work to be seen by patients. A fine example of such planning was the process which led to the creation of a stained-glass screen for the new entrance to the outpatients department at the Queen Elizabeth Hospital in Gateshead. The intricate abstract design was intended to absorb patients' attention and provide a relaxed atmosphere; but artists Mike Davis and Cate Watkinson were constrained by certain aesthetic limitations, including the following:

'Colourful, cheerful and reassuringly restful': patients' reaction to Graham Cowley's 1982 work for the out-patients department, Brompton Hospital, London.

● 'That the design should be balanced rather than specifically symmetrical, and although it could be dynamic, its movement should be contained within itself.

● That the colour range should be an analogous one, calm in feeling, with blue/blue-green as the only fully or nearly saturated colours. Of all the pure colours, blue is the favourite one in Western culture and its effect is calming, given the right context.

● That the screen should provide a focus for vision without being overdramatic or too dominant. The eye should be gently encouraged to scan it, and allowed to light on points of interest. Complementary colour contrasts, acute angular forms or sharp linear configurations should be avoided.' (13)

Of course the content of certain kinds of paintings can be especially beneficial to individual patients, even if done by amateurs. This can especially be the case where the artist has overcome a handicap in order to create the work. Ursula Hulme, who founded Conquest, a society for art for physically handicapped people, believes such works can often be of greater value than those done by professional artists. 'Someone disabled by a stroke can be encouraged by a painting which has been produced by a stroke sufferer,' she says. 'Equally, someone whose leg has been amputated may take courage if he or she sees a painting of dancers on the wall created by a patient who had both legs amputated after a road accident.' (14)

Images for children

Particular care obviously needs to be taken with the choice of subject and image when the visual arts are introduced into children's wards. Here consultation with nurses and play specialists is important. Giving scope for children's imagination to be used was the thinking behind work commissioned for Booth Hall Children's Hospital in Manchester. The bleak pre-fabricated 1960s building provided a gloomy setting for young people, and some of them had expressed their feelings through destructive behaviour, including using graffiti and tearing down posters put up by the nurses. Manchester's Hospital Arts team turned a corridor into a viewing point for space observation, with pictures of the solar system on the

Trip to the theatre: the spaceship lift at Wythenshawe Hospital, Manchester helps to reduce children's anxiety about their operations.

walls, and mobiles of planets hanging from the skylights. The artists also transformed a dingy nursing station into a control room of a space cruiser, with planets glowing through the 'window', and coloured mobiles of celestial bodies turning and twisting in the lightwells. The changes pleased the nurses, and were popular with the young patients - nurses say they have taken a pride in the artwork, and not damaged it. (15)

In other places the aim behind a commission targeted at children may be diversion, or the reduction of stress. This was the reason why, in the children's unit at Wythenshawe Hospital, also in Manchester, the theatre lift was turned into a spaceship by the Hospital Arts team. The idea came from sister Julie Gravett, after she played a game of 'let's pretend' in the lift with a particularly anxious child on his way to the operating theatre. Nowadays the children are usually taken up in the lift the day before their operation, so that on the day itself there is a different kind of journey to look forward to. The lift has become so well known that it is often the first thing children ask about when they are admitted to the hospital. (16)

Nora Gaston's watercolour sketch for the mural in the children's ward, Musgrave Park Hospital, Belfast.

A type of project particularly popular with children is one where they have a chance to participate, or where space is left for their own efforts to complement that of the commissioned work . In the paediatric unit at Wexham Park Hospital in Slough, for instance, children's paintings of animals are positioned alongside and complement the professionally painted murals, which depict story-book characters. At the Queen's Medical Centre in Nottingham, children were involved in deciding on an animal mascot and season for their ward, after which artists Lesley Hewitt and David Andrew, from Artistic Licence, created portals and overdoors for the wards that reflected the children's choices. At the Royal Victoria Hospital in Belfast, Ben Allen created a 50-foot long mural with the help of children, each of whom was invited to draw their own house and garden to help create the picture.

The Royal Victoria is in the Falls Road area of Belfast, and the fabric and image have suffered from the recent troubles. But they are not the only hospital to do so. Elsewhere in the city, artist Nora Gaston was commissioned to create a mural for the refurbished children's ward in Musgrave Park Hospital, a former American field hospital during the second world war, and still a mixture of Nissen huts and long corridors. The children's involvement in the mural work was rudely interrupted by the IRA, when the new ward was damaged by a bomb the day before the children were due to move into it. Nora Gaston recalls the moment: 'You can imagine the consternation, the doubts about whether the children should be there. Finally it was decided to go ahead.

So the murals were an integral part of this whole new beginning. They were important, and boosted morale at a time when it was badly needed.' Both staff and children were apparently pleased with their new surroundings, their reaction summed up by one young new arrival, who told his mother, 'This doesn't look like a hospital, it looks like a friendly place.' (17)

Hospices, health centres and clinics

With the arts now so well established in hospitals, it was to be expected that hospices would soon begin to explore what the arts could do for their dying patients. The main thrust of the work so far has been in the use of writers, mostly in projects initiated by Hospice Arts. (See pages 63 - 66 for a fuller description of their work.) But sculptors, painters and a textile artist have also worked in hospices, and students from a community music course in London have also become involved.

One well-documented example involved a ten-week residency by two sculptors, Marit Benthe Norheim and James Thrower, at St John's Hospice, Lancaster

Guitarist Hedley Kay at the bedside of a patient at St Joseph's Hospice, Hackney, London.

in 1987. A series of figurative sculptures was installed in the hospice bathroom. The theme chosen was that of a journey through memories and past experiences in order to approach a higher spiritual consciousness. Reactions to the work were very mixed, though in general they became more positive as the residency progressed. Significantly, the more positive reactions came from the in-patients, some of whom were able to get to know the artists, and to hear from them why these particular pieces had been made. While some day-patients, staff and visitors were critical of or uneasy about the work's power to challenge, several of the in-patients found it valuable to be able to talk about the impact of the artwork on their feelings, having already come to terms with their own imminent death.

The reaction of the matron at the hospice was particularly interesting, since she was initially sceptical, and thought when she first saw the sculptures that a dreadful mistake had been made. By the end of the residency she had become an eloquent defender of the work's value: 'These figures are so revealing, so expressive of human behaviour and present-day values, that it is not surprising many people find them painful, disturbing and even revolting. Some people have laughed at them, criticised them, ignored them, thought them obscene or ugly. Those who have had the courage to look and to question with open, unprejudiced minds have found them vaguely familiar and disturbingly true. They have been enriched by the experience, and some have grown, as I have, to find them a continuous source of self-revelation.' (18)

Mog Ball, a former director of Hospice Arts, emphasises the broader value of such projects: 'A growing body of artists who have personal contact with people who are dying and those who care for them can only help to open up this subject, and make it something that is discussed more easily. The evidence is growing that the arts can bring something to terminal care which might not otherwise be there.' (19)

Such work is only just beginning in health centres and clinics. Some of these small, under-funded places seem to epitomise the current state of public buildings, where no one seems to feel it is their responsibility to do anything about the lack of fresh air, the tatty chairs and magazines, the proliferation of notices and brusque instructions, the poor provision for parents with babies and young childen.

Like all spaces, they lend themselves to particular types of artwork which, along with better interior design and decoration, and the use of plants and flowers, can greatly improve their appearance. There is a need for people working there to take responsibility for making them more welcome and comforting spaces. Some are now beginning to do this, while the kind of approach that is being pioneered at Withymoor Surgery in Brierley Hill is likely to prove an invaluable model for others working in such places. (See page 70 for an account of this project.)

Artwork by patients at St Christopher's Hospice, Sydenham, south London.

New strategies

As the movement for arts projects and activities in health care has gained momentum, so a few enlightened district and regional health authorities have seen the value of planning an arts programme or strategy right across the authority, rather than adopting a piecemeal approach. Stockport Area Health Authority, for example, has recently asked Arts for Health to look at the entire provision across the district authority, and to come back with suggestions. Similarly, the North Western Regional Health Authority has committed itself to seeing that the arts play a fundamental part in every new capital scheme for the region, and has asked Arts for Health to be closely involved in the work.

As part of this initiative, Arts for Health is working with the project team to develop services at Bolton General Hospital. The hospital's re-development plan provides an excellent chance to look at the whole site and existing buildings, which include the old workhouse, laundry, ambulance station, boiler house and mental illness unit. Here Arts for Health can work with architects and planners to try to develop the whole of the exterior environment, as well as dealing with the planned art works and arts programme. Already it has pinpointed the need for welcoming entrances, improved landscaping, significant landmarks and signposting systems. It is planning an arts audit which will give plenty of opportunity for enhancement of the old buildings, sculpture, earthworks, decorative footpaths, colourful paving, an artworks trail, interesting lighting in the grounds, a camouflaging of the car parks, a children's playground and a garden of tranquillity. There will also be an assessment and re-siting of the hospital's collection of artistic artefacts.

Such collaboration at an early stage between arts personnel and architects, planners and designers is essential if the arts are going to play a central role in new health care building programmes. Here it is important that we see the visual arts in a broad sense, so that, as Howard Goodman has recently suggested, it includes everything that patients see or touch during their period of care. 'All the items that surround the small world of the patient have been chosen by someone, although the criteria which are involved in the process may be difficult to understand. Often it is simply which works the best, but more likely it is which is the cheapest, or most easily obtainable. Rarely are the criteria concerned with what it looks like, whether it is well designed, or how it relates to its neighbours.' He argues that such decisions about even small items affect how patients feel about the quality of care they are receiving. 'A blue cup on a green saucer, cutlery that would put the local greasy spoon caff to shame, bed curtains that clash horribly with the counterpane... and the patient soon begins to wonder whether the same attention to detail is given to the life-support machine that he may soon depend upon.' (20)

Already there are signs that such approaches are being adopted. For example, at St Luke's Hospital in Bradford, where an arts programme is being initiated as part of a Caring Arts project, there are plans for textile designs and colourways to be commissioned for duvet covers, bed screens and window curtains in the paediatric department and child development centre. At the new Wansbeck General Hospital, due to open in Ashington, Northumberland in November 1993, the theme chosen for all the arts projects - based on the four elements - will be integrated into all aspects of the hospital's design, from curtain fabric to special floor effects. (21)

Such detailed planning was important in the case of St Mary's, Newport, the new low-energy hospital on the Isle of Wight, where even the colour of the bedspreads in the wards was part of the overall design plan. The plans, proposals and illustrations, which were shown to everyone involved, demonstrated how every aspect of the arts, craft and design could complement the form and function of the hospital. Floors, walls, ceilings and lighting were considered for their potential for design, decoration and art. Three themes were chosen to reflect aspects of the island, which were then reflected in the interior design, the landscape design and the art works within the building.

The planning was also done in close conjunction with the architect Richard Burton, of Ahrends, Burton and Koralek. His interest in the arts, his sensitivity as an artist, and his conviction as a former patient enabled him to recognise that something fundamental was missing from hospital buildings. He made it clear that his guiding aim was to make a hospital where the architecture, art, craft and landscape would play a beneficial role in people's lives. The integration of the artwork and the high quality of the interior owes much to his skills and vision, and to those of the interior designer, Stephen Nicoll. (See page 84 for a more detailed description of the Isle of Wight initiative.)

Another model for the future is the new Chelsea and Westminster Hospital, due to open in London in 1993 at an estimated total cost of £206m. Arts for Health was commissioned to develop the arts programme, and recommended the theme of 'Theatre for Health', emphasising the relationship between theatre and healing: this theme has been agreed on for this breathtaking open-plan building, where everyone is at once actor and audience.

An artist's impression of the 'Theatre for Health' theme for the Chelsea and Westminster Hospital, London.

Despite the many exciting ideas, some elements could have been different. It would have been better to integrate the arts from the first planning meeting, as in the Isle of Wight, instead of two and a half years into the process. Then there is the funding question. The Special Trustees of Westminster and Roehampton Hospitals have provided a generous initial budget of £200,000. However, in order to complete the visual arts side, and to equip the performance space, it has proved necessary to fundraise from sponsors.

In this day and age it is horrifying that, with a new building of this kind, there is no mechanism or encouragement to put money aside. There is, however, a growing interest in the 'percent for art' idea, by which a proportion of the capital cost of buildings and environmental schemes is set aside for commissions to artists and craftspeople. Such a scheme is applied in many European countries and across the United States, where it is mandatory in 21 states and 91 cities. Its effect has been to make visible improvements to the built environment, to increase patronage of the arts, and to enable new money to be injected into the arts. Had 1% of the capital cost been set aside in the case of the Chelsea and Westminster Hospital, around £2.06m would have been available. This would have allowed a properly resourced and more ambitious arts project to have developed, and left the arts personnel free to get on with the business of developing and maintaining a top-quality range of works and activities, instead of expending valuable time and energy trying to raise money.

Such experiences underline how important it is for money to be set aside for the arts from the earliest planning stage. In 1990 the Arts Council recommended that the government adopt percent for art policies within the NHS capital programme. In 1991 Tim Renton, then the arts minister, supported the idea of 1% for art during a visit to the new Princess Royal Hospital in Hayward's Heath in Sussex. (22) However, until now the government has passed the buck, although the Department of Health is in agreement with the idea in principle - and its new building in Leeds has a percent scheme in it. Meanwhile, as long as the notion remains a voluntary one, decisions will have to be made at local level, leaving it to the vision and courage of individuals to introduce such a scheme. Until there is a sum included within the budget costs of all new and refurbished health building programmes, any collaboration between client, design team and artists will continue to be a make-do-and-mend solution.

Chapter 4
Working Together

'What does a hospital such as the Royal, with an excellent reputation worldwide, need with an artist? What function will this person perform? Will someone please explain?'

Letter in the Belfast Telegraph, *1989*

Everyone should have access to the arts. It should be more than just a cosmetic exercise. Morale is often low in the health service, and staff lacking in self-confidence and self-esteem. Getting patients and staff involved in arts activities can make people feel better, produce new ideas, change attitudes, and lead to further initiatives.

Many of the projects set up in recent years in hospitals, hospices, day-care centres, residential homes and other places have unlocked new worlds for artists and participants alike. Patients who have had no active involvement in the arts have found new skills and unexpected talents, and a way of combating the isolation and loss of identity that so often accompanies illness or an enforced separation from everyday life. Where staff have been involved, they have seen their patients in a new light, as well as having their own attitude to the arts challenged.

Equally, some artists have found that the experience has enriched and deepened their own artistic development. Yet such partnerships have rarely been plain sailing, even where the funding and organisational difficulties have been overcome. The presence of an artist has often resulted in a conflict of values - not just in relation to artistic tastes and standards, but also the potential of the arts to assist with healing.

Artists-in-residence

Some of the most successful projects in the visual arts have come out of long-term residencies, especially where these have led to the establishment of an arts team. In such circumstances the artist has had the time to nurture the development of people who may be new to an activity, unsure about their ability to revive a former skill, or hampered by their physical or mental condition. Lucy Milton, director of the Artists' Agency, which has arranged a wide variety of residencies over the last ten years, believes this kind of contact between artists and the public is especially important in health settings: 'People there often feel frightened, impotent and isolated,' she says. 'Artists sharing their creative practice with them can enable people who do not have access to decision-making in their environment to realise their inner feelings, and thus develop and communicate

new understandings of themselves, their lives and the world. Creating their own work encourages them to make positive decisions and develop the confidence to tackle change. It also enables them to share their ideas with others, leading to more positive relationships with the outside world.' (1)

Many of the artists who have undertaken such residencies have stressed how important it is that patients see them as being separate from medical staff, and treat their studio or working space as a place unconnected with medicine or treatment. Alan Vaughan was resident artist for 18 months in the psychiatric department of the North Tyneside General Hospital in North Shields, working in a large room within the hospital.

'The art studio was a place where the patients could establish an identity - both physically, in that they could create a personal space where they could leave paintings, experiments, objects or even just a haphazard mess; and mentally, in that the atmosphere and the very nature of the work was conducive to personal reassessment, to finding new directions and priorities, and the self-belief needed to make significant changes to their lives. The room gradually became something of an artistic haven, where patients could reclaim and keep hold of their sense of individuality while being processed in an alien and impersonal environment.'

Several patients testified to the positive effect of their time in the studio. One man told the artist: 'Your room was the only place where I could constructively pass the time whilst at the same time create something new. This gave me both a hope for the future, and a feeling that I was getting better. The studio certainly provided a place where a bored, restless mind could be uplifted and inspired.' A woman patient, who described herself as someone 'who has to be doing or keeping busy', was equally enthusiastic. 'I felt I wasn't just a patient sitting around, I had actually achieved a work of art. I was very uplifted by the experience of actually doing and completing work which was started.' For some, the work was an antidote to apathy and depression. As another woman admitted: 'It's the first time I've smiled here.' (2)

Artists have always stressed that participation in such projects is voluntary, that people are made fully aware of the opportunities available, but are under no pressure to attend. It is also made clear that individuals are free to follow their own interests at their own speed. Ruth Priestley is artist-in-residence at the Royal Victoria Hospital in Belfast, and has worked with patients on the wards doing mosaic and textile activities. 'The ward workshops are a good tonic for the patients,' she says. 'Those taking part can be creative without pressure or competition; they enjoy forgetting about themselves for a while.' This latter point was illustrated by one male participant, who had been unable to pass urine after an operation. This had made him anxious, and no treatment seemed to help. Persuaded to join one of the workshops, he was able to overcome his problem immediately afterwards. (3)

The need to feel secure is especially important for psychiatric patients. Sculptress Annie Cattrell was artist-in-residence at the Royal Edinburgh Hospital in 1990/91. One of her first concerns was to create a relaxed atmosphere in her studio: many patients had been in the hospital for 30 or 40 years, had become institutionalised, and were very anxious about anything new. A management report two-thirds of the way through the residency made it clear that the initial anxieties had been overcome: 'The past eight months have seen attendance at the studio go from strength to strength...Individuals have relaxed and become motivated to express themselves, to use their imagination and be creative within "art".' Staff reported that patients who started out by saying 'I can't do it,' ended up saying, 'I can't believe what I've done.' (4)

Once in Annie Cattrell's studio, patients had plenty of choice: they were able to do plaster casting, use acrylic paints, create mosaics from old crockery and tiles, use recycled and natural materials to form three-dimensional work, or make use of a typewriter. The artist tried to encourage them to use their own experience for inspiration, perhaps to represent their childhood or home environment, or their present ideas and interests. 'It's an activity they can remember, and one which helps them delve into their past lives,' she says. 'Although at first most residents

had little confidence in their own ability, this anxiety slowly disappeared once they realised that there was no pressure to produce end-results.' (5)

The hospital management report suggested that the therapeutic, recreational and social benefits to the patients were quite considerable, prolonging their attention and concentration spans, giving them a new sense of achievement and self-worth, and improving their interpersonal skills. Artist Ian Hughes, who followed Annie Cattrell for the year 1991/92, put this kind of result down to the nature of the shared experience between artist and patient. Halfway through his residency he confessed to being impressed and overcome by the enthusiasm and ability of both residents and staff: 'Some of the results of residents' work are genuinely exciting to me as an artist, and hopefully there has been an exchange the other way,' he said. 'I have come to regard the residents as fellow artists, each with special individual talents and skills. They are also my friends, and often they will enter my studio to see and discuss what I'm working on. The studio provides us with a very healthy creative environment where we treat each other with mutual respect.' (6)

Evidence of the impact of these residencies can be found in the reports on individual patients prepared by the coordinating artists' agency in Edinburgh, Artlink. One young man with low self-esteem had previously been disparaging about his own drawing and painting. With the artists' encouragement he had worked on a mural, taken pride in the result, and revealed a gift for poetry. Another man, one of the most talented of the patients, told Ian Hughes that no one had actually sat down with him before and taught him how to draw and paint. An older woman progressed from painting flower images all the time, to expanding her work to include butterflies, animals and abstract paintings. She eventually wrote to Artlink saying that art was the only important thing in her life, that she didn't know how to pass the time without being involved in it, and asking if Ian Hughes could come every day.

In Edinburgh, as with other residencies, many staff have been drawn in to activities and, like their patients, have been able to discover talents that in many cases they didn't know they possessed. A benefit of this wider involvement is the effect it has had on the views of nurses, ward sisters and other staff about the value of art, and about artists as a breed. Stereotypical ideas and prejudices have usually been changed, or at least challenged, once staff have got to know artists on a personal level, and begun to see the potential or the impact of their work, whether on the environment or on patients.

Changing attitudes

Ruth Priestley is one of several artists who have had to fight for recognition of what they are doing. Of the project at the Royal Victoria Hospital in Belfast, she says: 'It has made people more aware of different forms of art, and is helping break down limiting ideas about what art is, and where it belongs in different environments.' The main difficulty, she feels, has been one of trust. 'People make all sorts of wrong judgements about artists: that they're lazy, they don't have any money, they take drugs, and so on. The first year was spent convincing staff that I was not going to make a mess, that I knew what I was doing.' A project she planned for the main entrance proved to be a particular bone of contention. 'A nurse manager thought I had gone crazy when I suggested doing mosaics on four pillars. It took weeks of meetings, examples and designs to convince her that mosaic was a beautiful medium. Now that one pillar is complete she is delighted with it, and I have received an apology.' (7)

Artist Peter Messer noticed a more gradual change while he was working on murals in Crawley Hospital and the Princess Royal Hospital in Hayward's Heath, both in Sussex: 'In both cases, the attitudes moved slowly from amused scepticism and indifference to enthusiasm and delight as the work progressed. Much of this was due to the comparative rarity of the sight of a professional artist at work. At the Princess Royal especially, the staff became very proprietorial and proud of their mural. I was able to incorporate a number of their suggestions for details into the painting, which increased their sense of ownership.' (8)

Among other obstacles artists have had to contend with are unnecessary bureaucracy, institutional inertia or a preference for the tried and trusted.

Artist David Goard, who spent a year at Plummer Court, a drug and alcohol rehabilitation unit in Newcastle-upon-Tyne, says: 'The artist can be seen as a threat to existing practices. All institutions have their bureaucracies, but health care has got it in spades. It's a sad and unfortunate situation, and often damaging in a pernicious sort of way. Obviously the artist must be sensitive to the structure within which he or she operates, yet also maintain some distance from it - a delicate balancing act.' Mary Paterson, who spent a year as arts coordinator at the new Cannock Community Hospital in Staffordshire, says: 'Because art can sometimes be controversial in an organisation like the NHS, projects may simply be abandoned by staff, rather than have them cause a stir.'(9)

In other places artists have had to come to grips with a difference in priorities between themselves and other staff, notably occupational therapists. Frances Broomfield, artist-in-residence in the geriatric ward in Ealing Hospital in west London, has found herself caught in just such a dilemma. 'The occupational therapy department are looking for things to display on the wall, whereas for the elderly patients themselves, it is just the process of working that they find enjoyable,' she says. 'There isn't always an end-product, but you have to try to please both parties: I have to show some finished work in order to keep the department happy.' (10)

Few artists involved in a residency or an arts team have found it easy to strike the right balance between their own work and that which they are doing with or for others. It has also often been a struggle to maintain the integrity of their own work. David Goard highlights some of the dilemmas arising out of his work at Plummer Court in Newcastle: 'Being on view, as a resident artist often is, may be a motivation to be particularly productive. This is a dodgy area, though, since there may be less time to contemplate than one is used to. There may also be the subconscious desire to please, rather than be true to one's own art. Working in an area where people are physically or mentally ill also creates a pressure or sense of responsibility to be positive in outlook, not only in everyday dealings with people, but also in one's creations. It's debatable whether this is a good or bad thing.' (11)

North Tyneside Art Studio, North Shields, offers space and materials for local people with mental illness or addiction problems.

Side panel of tryptych by Alan Vaughan in the Department of Psychiatry, North Tyneside General Hospital.

Several artists believe that working alongside patients has had a marked effect on the content and quality of their own work. While he was at the Royal Edinburgh Hospital, Ian Hughes was preparing an exhibition of portraits of victims and survivors of the Holocaust, and found the patients' comments on his work illuminating. 'They frequently make very telling and meaningful criticisms. It is a two-way process; we are learning from each other. My work is being affected by working here - I would be a poor artist if I wasn't inspired by my environment.' (12) Alan Vaughan, recalling his North Tyneside residency, suggests how an artist's work can be altered when there is a real empathy with patients. 'I had experienced many of the problems of poverty, bad housing and lack of esteem in others' eyes which were particularly relevant to this group. I think my own work was enhanced as I became more sensitive to, and conscious of, the honesty, vulnerability, and yet great strength of the patients, who were often facing problems and questions most of us might recognise, but avoid and bury.' (13)

For some artists, the residency provided a challenge to their own thinking about public and private art.

Heather Parnell, artist-in-residence at Llandough Hospital in South Glamorgan during 1990/91, found herself having to deal with this difficult issue: 'The complexities of personally producing artworks for the hospital has raised many questions which for me remain unresolved. Efforts to produce work which contains personal ideas whilst maintaining accessibility for a broad public has forced me to question which elements of "myself" are most appropriate, and which personal ideas I want to make public in this hospital context.' (14)

A few artists were also affected by their first real contact with public attitudes to the arts. While hospital staff could often prove limited in their outlook and lacking in imagination, other sections of the public sometimes shook the artist's preconceptions. For Peter Messer, contact with the public at the two Sussex hospitals where he worked on murals was something of a revelation: 'Among the many gains for me has been the sense that interest in visual things goes very deep among people whom it is very easy to dismiss as "the six-pack and video culture". In fact, there seems to be a basic, common, shy hunger for art among precisely those most disenfranchised culturally. They are apologetic about liking things, feeling it not quite for them.' (15)

Into the community

One of the most encouraging signs of the value of this kind of arts activity has been the way several residencies or projects have resulted in the setting-up of permanent organisations, to continue and develop similar work in the community. Here some of the fundamental aims have been to help with former patients' rehabilitation; to assist them in their progress towards greater independence; or simply to continue to offer them access to the arts.

One of the longest established of such places is the Art Studio in Sunderland. This pioneering scheme began in 1986, when two visual artists were given a one-year placement by the Artists' Agency, to work in the East End of the town with former residents of Cherry Knowle Psychiatric Hospital, and others 'at risk' in the area. Artists Derek Hill and Chris Sell established an open access studio, with facilities for painting, drawing, sculpture and print-making. In order to attract clients, they initially spent time at local centres, doing their own work. Later, within the studio, their clients were encouraged to work alongside the artists and each other, pursuing their individual lines.

'We worked with people from all sorts of backgrounds, some of whom had been through very hard times,' Chris Sell recalls. 'But from the start we had a policy of treating those who came to the studio as people, not patients or cases. I learnt what a lot of support there is around for something that people feel they can trust. Some of the users did wonderful work, and we formed a community with a lot of self-respect.' The studio became so popular that it soon had to move to larger premises. Nowadays, with space for 50 artists to work, it is no longer limited to people 'at risk', but has become a general community resource. (16)

More recently, the North Tyneside Art Studio, established in 1991, grew out of Alan Vaughan's residency in the psychiatric department of the North Tyneside General Hospital. It provides space and materials for 30 people having mental health or

mental illness or addiction problems, most of whom are living at home or in sheltered housing. Places are allocated by recommendation from mental health workers, social workers, or by self-recommendation with backing from a health professional. The studio aims to be part of the mental health service for the district, and a focus for creative activity that will link up with other artistic projects, schemes and people.

The arts centre in Darlington has been the focus of a similar project, an innovative care-in-the-community scheme set up by the Artists' Agency in 1985. The studio space and artist-in-residence at the centre followed on from a residency at the town's Aycliffe Hospital, a long-stay hospital for people with learning difficulties. It is used by former Aycliffe residents returning to the community, as well as people attending day centres and training centres.

Sculptor Annalise Smith, the second of three visual artists to have been in residence, says her aim during her two years there was to promote values and freedoms threatened by the institutionalising process, and to assert the importance of creativity. 'What I had taken for granted as an artistic reality - an acceptance of the whole person, and a belief in the creative worth of the individual - was called into question by the institutionalised view, which denies the creative integrity and freedom of the individual. I have tried to work alongside the group as an artist and an equal, to provide a lively, stimulating environment, a time and space for the exploration of already rich imaginations.' (17)

Close links were soon formed between the artists in the hospital and those in the arts centre, leading to several fruitful collaborative projects that combined music and the visual arts. In 1989 the local health authority, impressed with the impact the work was having, took over the Darlington project. Geoff Nichol, the authority's district general manager, had become convinced that when people were able to develop their creative abilities, it had a positive effect on other areas of their lives: 'The project in Darlington and Aycliffe has demonstrated this beyond doubt, and it is enormously satisfying to see the measurable improvement in the quality of life enjoyed by those of our residents and clients who

Members of START Studios on a day out, and the resulting 'Head for the Hills' mosaic, at the Manchester Royal Infirmary.

have participated in the project activity.' Ian Patterson, formerly monitoring officer for Darlington's community nursing scheme, was similarly impressed: 'I found it most encouraging as the months went by to observe people develop and grow into individuals who could say "Yes, I will do that" or "No, I want to do something different". Seeing the benefits has made me realise that art, sculpture and music are so much more than leisure pursuits.'(18)

Such projects usually develop according to the needs of the community they serve, particularly when the programme is long-standing. Such was certainly the case with START studios in Manchester, a community arts centre catering for patients who have returned to the community. While working for the Hospital Arts team, START's founder and director artist Langley Brown had developed a particular relationship with the psychiatric department of Manchester Royal Infirmary. With the arts team's photographer, Jack Sutton, he went regularly with patients to the Peak District in Derbyshire, painting, sketching and photographing the landscape. The result was a magnificent mosaic mural entitled 'Head for the Hills'. This was created on site in the psychiatric day hospital by the group, who invited other patients, staff and visitors to take part as they were passing through or waiting. From this and other similar events, the idea evolved for an arts programme based in the community for psychiatric patients who had been discharged, and for whom worthwhile activities and occupations were scarce.

START - originally known as Sheltered Training in Arts - began in 1986. Now housed in a former hospital

building in the Victoria Park area of Manchester, its rooms provide space for people to get involved with drawing, painting, design, textiles, photography, pottery, mosaic, stained glass, picture framing, woodwork, and music. It has a membership of 60, accepted through medical referrals - although recently it has become so popular it is having to consider closing its referral list for a while.

The centre is publicised as a place where people recovering from mental illness 'find that the arts are not merely a powerful antidote to loneliness, but also a significant means of self-fulfilment and of giving pleasure to others'. Langley Brown is keen that people coming to the centre should leave their medical history behind. 'We don't call it therapy, we call it art,' he says. 'We're not interested in people's medical history. Illness is a shared negative experience, whereas we offer a shared positive experience through the arts.' (19)

Yet START also makes it clear that it's not just the process that is important for the members. Part of the work is the fostering of partnerships with

Staff creche at the Manchester Royal Infirmary: the children's paintings later inspired START Studios members' design for a play area at the hospital.

professional artists to undertake paid project work in a wide variety of community settings. Recent environmental art projects have included work in a wildlife garden, in schools, and in a local children's hospital. Members are also given advice and assistance in organising exhibitions and carrying through commissions, while a few of the more established members run classes, and are paid on a therapeutic earnings basis.

The personal, social and artistic gains for those who come to START are plain to see. Now other north-west area health authorities, such as Stockport, Salford and Bolton, are looking seriously at the START model for other reasons. Research on the effects of START showed that it produced a significant reduction in the use of in-patient and day hospital facilities, and that members were referred to fewer health professionals than before. This had the effect of freeing much needed resources for more acute cases. The researchers also found that START may have helped to reduce the risk of relapse. As Langley Brown summarises it: 'The people we work with are too busy to go back to hospital.' The NHS Health Advisory Service (which reports directly to the Secretary of State and to health authorities about health service provision in the UK) in its

Inspectorate Report (1991) named START under the heading 'Good Practice, Exceptional and Applicable Elsewhere'.

At a time when psychiatric hospitals are being closed down and a growing number of patients being discharged into the community, projects like START should play an increasingly important part in providing alternative resources.

All these residencies and projects with participation at their core have substantially increased the number of people able to be personally involved in the visual arts simply for their own pleasure. It has, for many of the artists and arts administrators involved, confirmed their view that everyone has some form of creativity in them if they have the chance to find the right medium through which to express it. That more and more health care staff have seen the therapeutic and medical benefits that can follow, is shown by the increasing number of hospitals or health authorities that are prepared to allocate funds to enable people to participate in arts activities of this kind, believing them to be life-enhancing, an essential part of creative caring, and cost-effective. It is hoped that other health authorities will come to realise the benefits that the arts can bring to everyone within their care.

An Enriching Process

Bellarmine Hospital Arts
Project, Glasgow

'I think at first they wondered who this smart-alec artist was, coming in to brighten the place up. But they soon realised that I was a normal person, not someone with Art on.'

The staff at Kirklands Hospital for mentally handicapped people could be forgiven for being initially wary of Stephen Beddoe. A graduate from the Glasgow School of Art, he was the Bellarmine Arts Project's first artist-in-residence in the hospital. Was he just going to barge in and tell them what was best for them and the residents?

It didn't work out like that. His brief was to identify a number of sites around the hospital where art could be introduced. He chose to create a colourful mural in the new staff dining area, and this soon attracted the interest of staff. Patients also began to come to see what he was doing, and started to produce drawings and paintings themselves. 'It broke the ice once I started working in front of them,' he remembers.

That was three years ago. Today there are three artists working in the hospital full- or part-time, their presence pretty much taken for granted. Katherine Pearson, the current artist-in-residence, notices the difference: 'The groundwork has been done, people know us, you no longer have to run around asking for things from the technical staff. Instead of "What do you want that for?" it's become "How can we help?"'

The artists' work at Kirklands is just one strand of the Bellarmine Hospital Arts Project, a collaboration between Lanarkshire Health Board and the Bellarmine Arts Association which has brought Scottish artists into contact with hospital residents, and other people with special needs. The resulting arts activities have taken place in a number of hospitals in the Glasgow area, and in the association's arts centre in Bellarmine School, south Glasgow.

One of the unusual aspects of the project is the involvement of young artists, most of them postgraduate or undergraduate art students from Glasgow, Dundee and Canterbury. Tom Chambers, one of the association's founding members, and current coordinator of the hospital project, also works part-time at the Glasgow School of Art. He feels the project has given the students a different perspective on the function of art, complementing the view of art as commodity. 'Most of them were producing things, or planning to do so. We were looking for an alternative to that, and trying to raise the issue of community arts as regeneration. It wasn't a question of painting political posters, but increasing awareness of how art belongs to the roots of the community.'

The association's first project involved work on one of Glasgow's peripheral estates, with the Saturday club for the mentally handicapped in Pollock. Since then, the art students have worked with different special needs groups, including elderly people, the mentally handicapped and mentally ill, the visually and hearing impaired, and the long-term unemployed. Among the skills they have taught them are those needed for photography, bronze casting, screen printing, ceramics, stained glass, and working in clay, plaster and cement.

'Making the object is not just a private thing,' Tom Chambers argues. 'The interaction is part of the art, it's an enriching process in itself.' The students have been signing up in increasing numbers to work with residents at the annual summer school held in Kirklands, and in 1992 in summer projects in Glasgow and Ayrshire. Four years on, a scheme that started with a few students from the Sculpture department at Glasgow has now drawn in many others from departments such as Painting, Graphics, Print-making, Environmental Art, and Textiles.

Among those who have attended the sessions at Bellarmine are some of the more independent residents of Kirklands Hospital, who, until the recent cuts arising from the poll-tax crisis, have been regularly bussed to the arts centre. Having become quite accustomed to working with artists in this way, it was perhaps easier for them to adapt to the idea of having artists in their own hospital.

Kirklands is an attractive new hospital in the town of Bothwell, eight miles south of Glasgow. It was built to replace the former red-brick 'asylum' that had stood on the site since the last century. Opened in the early 1980s, the new building is designed on the model of a village, the traditional wards being replaced by low-level, beige-walled 'cottages' dotted around the grounds, each with its own garden area. The patients, known as 'residents', are grouped according to their levels of need and capability. While some can wander freely round the grounds by themselves, others need constant supervision.

From the beginning, the building division of the Scottish Health Service Common Services Agency saw scope for including artwork as part of the architecture of the hospital. Examples of the residents' work are to be found in different parts of the main block. In the corridors several of their paintings and sculptures are on display; in one of the inner courtyards stand a terracotta planter, and a cement seat with animals for legs; in the sensory training area is a series of wall hangings. Some of these works have been done in conjunction with the hospital staff, notably the occupational therapists.

Fiona Dean's 'The Whale' in the central meeting place at Kirklands Hospital, Lanarkshire.

In the centre of the 'village', which acts as an informal meeting place, there stands a large whale and fish sculpture, created out of cement, stainless steel and bronze by a previous Bellarmine artist-in-residence, Fiona Dean. Much of the work done by the artists at Kirklands has been fashioned with the particular needs of the residents in mind. In the 'sensory courtyard' next to one of the corridors in the main block, for example, artist Tom McGarvey has created an ingenious red, yellow and blue 'sensory chair'. On this piece of sound sculpture residents can sit and, if they so wish, make musical sounds on the tubular components of the sculpture, or identify the colours used by the artist. Helpfully, the chair is also accessible to those who are confined to wheelchairs.

Participation is central to all the work being done at Kirklands. 'We didn't want the artists to produce art without involvement with the residents,' Tom Chambers says. How, though, do the artists manage to achieve a balance between their community art and their own development as artists?

Tom McGarvey, who has been associated with Bellarmine for seven years and with Kirklands for five, has worked with many kinds of special needs groups. He finds no problem in doing so during his three days a week at Kirklands. 'I'm not too precious about my own work,' he says. 'It's important to open up to everything the

residents put forward: collaboration is more important. If you're working with a community, you've got to show respect, otherwise it's patronising.'

Katherine Pearson is the third artist-in-residence at the hospital, now nearly halfway through her year. She feels that any distinction between her personal and community work is unnecessary. 'It's a great environment to work in,' she says. 'I get a tremendous buzz working with the residents; I really like their work, and helping to meet their need to do something better. I don't want my own work to be separate, I want it to reflect my being here - and I want the workshops I do with the residents to be about the hospital, to include imagery that is relevant to them.'

With this in mind she is about to embark on a photo screen-printing project, in which residents will be encouraged to select an image that reflects life in their cottage, and then help her to produce the end-product. 'I want them to be involved,' she says. In another project, they will be invited to make a journey round the hospital, choosing and helping to make plaster casts of pieces of ground that they like, which will then be included in an installation in the main therapy and recreation area.

The two projects will, she feels, reflect both the positive and the negative side of life in hospital. 'There's always two sides; protection can be either caring or imprisoning, and I'm interested in exploring that duality,' she suggests. 'Every day the residents are still here, and that makes you question this type of institution, such as who decides on things. I'm trying to deal with these kind of questions through the work.'

The Kirklands artists liaise frequently with staff in the occupational therapy unit. But although they believe that their work has increased the residents' skills and social

'We didn't want the artists to produce art without involvement with the Kirklands residents.'

contacts, and given them a sense of achievement, they are clear that they are not involved in art therapy, and that any assessment of the medical benefits is outside their field. 'We have nothing to do with art therapy,' Katherine Pearson says. 'Our job is simply to assess the extension of their ability to create visual images, and the extension of their understanding.'

The process of learning has not been in one direction only. Tom Chambers believes that the residents' work has often affected that of the artists, generally making it simpler. Tom McGarvey acknowledges such an influence - and admits to stealing some spaceship imagery from one of the residents. 'My own work is certainly based on being in this place,' he says. The art students also say they are influenced by the boldness and expressiveness of the residents' work.

Above and opposite page
Artwork by visiting artists
at Kirklands Hospital.

At present the three artists are fortunate enough to have their own premises - a decent-sized block from the former building, left by the health board specifically for their use as an art workshop. Here there is ample studio space to work in, as well as enough room for storing materials and work in progress. However, at present only some of the residents are able to use the building, because health and safety standards prevent others, for instance those in wheelchairs, from doing so. However, money has been set aside to upgrade the facilities, to allow residents more access. 'If it's open access, then residents can just be in here and potter,' Katherine Pearson says. 'Some of them anyway just want to sit and have the company, which is fine.' In one area of the studio, Stephen Beddoe is working on a series of screenprints. Both he and Tom McGarvey now use the art workshop as a base, and spend some of each week working outside the hospital, with other special needs groups. The screenprints have emerged from another Bellarmine Hospital Arts Project, this one based at Stonehouse, a small village a few miles south of Bothwell.

Here the focus is on putting children from the local primary school in touch with the village hospital, the old TB hospital built in the 1940s which, to some local people, still has a stigma attached to it. The concept of hospital design has been introduced and will be the focus of work, with input from architects and planners.

If you want to get
ahead...an art class at
Kirklands Hospital.

As visiting artist, Stephen Beddoe has been working in the school one day a week, showing the children how to design and execute a mural, so that they can eventually create one themselves for the local hospital. 'We're trying to forge more of a bond between the village and the hospital, and to show the children that it's not a mysterious place,' he explains. 'The kids have loved it.'

The children have been involved in imagining what a perfect hospital might be like - suggestions have included the provision of swimming pools, ponds, garden walks, a maze, play areas, a mural, and sculpture. Subsequently they have been constructing proposal boards designed to show how the public areas could be transformed.

The underlying idea of the project, which has been funded by BP Exploration, Strathclyde Regional Authority, and the Carnegie UK Trust, is to introduce the children to the idea of making art which represents their locality, and which is accessible to those with special needs. The subject matter for the screenprints came about by courtesy of a reminiscence group organised by the local doctor, who had in his possession some 200 glass slides showing how this once-famous weaving village looked at the turn of the century.

The Bellarmine Hospital Arts Project has also acted as an agency for artists in the area. In the Western Infirmary in Glasgow, for instance, it was responsible for appointing artist William McCall, a student at the Glasgow School of Art. His initial painting on a water theme for a stairwell in the hospital was followed up by the circulation of a questionnaire inviting comments, and an invitation to staff, patients and their families to make suggestions as to how the whole three-storey stairwell space could be used for art, and be refurbished. Elsewhere in the hospital, the project commissioned a striking, blue stained glass window from Leslie MacFie, a recent graduate from the Glasgow School of Art, who had set up and operated a stained glass workshop at Bellarmine.

Tom Chambers believes that the hospital arts project's efforts to widen the horizons of young artists have been successful. 'You'd think in the art schools that this type of art would be marginalised,' he says. 'But no, it's attracted a lot of positive thinking amongst the students.' According to Stephen Beddoe, the perceptions of this kind of work by art students has changed. 'Not long ago it wasn't the trendy thing to do, people thought you must be a failure if you were a hospital artist. But there's no stigma now: it's accepted, it's even hip to be one.'

Chapter 5
Music, Dance and Drama

'And it came to pass, when the evil spirit from God was upon Saul, that David took an harp, and played with his hand: so Saul was refreshed, and was well, and the evil spirit departed from him.'

I Samuel 16:23

Ill-health has many drawbacks. For some people, to be unable to go to performances of dance, music or theatre can be a tremendous deprivation. For others, the disappointment at not being able to carry on playing an instrument or going to movement, dance or drama classes can be equally frustrating. Yet though there are still plenty of places where culture for patients means television and the annual Christmas singalong, there is a growing recognition that the performing arts have a potentially valuable role to play in enhancing patients' lives, whether they are confined to being members of an audience, or, as is increasingly the case, being encouraged to participate. This recognition has led to an explosion of work in health care settings, of which the examples in this chapter are inevitably only a tiny proportion.

The power of music

It's often said that, of all the art-forms used in health care, music is the one that has the power to affect patients most easily and most profoundly. Since Roman times it has been shown that music can affect the physical functions of the body, especially the pulse rate. This has sometimes been used to reduce dependence on drugs or the need for premedication before anaesthetics. Less scientifically, there is a consensus that a performance of suitable music can lessen tension and stress when people are ill. (1)

Certainly it was the first of the performing arts to be used in any systematic way in British hospitals. In 1948 a group of people, concerned about the isolation of patients, took a wind-up gramophone and a batch of 78 rpm records into a psychiatric hospital. The good response led directly to the setting up of the Council for Music in Hospitals, with its aim of bringing high-quality music to people who are too old, sick or handicapped to attend a concert or show. It was soon realised that live music, with its scope for participation by patients, was likely to prove even more beneficial than recorded music, and so concerts by professional musicians were organised. In the last 20 years the growth has been phenomenal, from around 100 a year to 2,800 in 1991.

Nowadays some 200 musicians of all kinds perform for the Council to a wide variety of audiences, including psychiatric patients, long-stay elderly patients, people with learning difficulties, nursing home and rest home residents, profoundly handicapped youngsters, and terminally ill patients. They play not just classical music but folk, jazz, pop, blues, world music - indeed, any kind of music that may be thought to be appropriate for a particular group of patients, whether they are in a hospital, hospice, day-care centre, or children's ward of a hospital. The testimonies of patients and staff in hundreds of these institutions show clearly how warmly such performances are welcomed, and how they can play their part in the healing process. 'The concerts enrich the patients' lives, they make them feel that people care,' says Sylvia Lindsay, the Council's director. 'They're a stimulation to the most apathetic patients: we get many cases of people speaking for the first time for many months after hearing a concert. Music is an incomparable means of communication; people often relate to music when words have lost their meaning.' (2)

Nella Kerr, who runs the Scottish branch of the Council, has found that health care staff often see an entirely different side of a patient's character during a performance. She remembers one of many examples of the power of music to alter behaviour dramatically: 'A ward sister at the Edinburgh Royal Infirmary, while watching a patient singing and nearly dancing out of her wheelchair, laughingly told me: "That woman usually swears at us from the minute she wakes in the morning until she goes to sleep at night."' (3)

Musicians have similar stories to tell. Ian Edwards, who visits around 100 hospitals a year with his music partner Jennifer Rice, is one of the many professionals who have seen the dramatic effects of music at first hand. 'The music itself can cheer and excite, calm and soothe, and encourage a whole range of emotions,' he says. 'Often it results in a real breakthrough, when other treatment and therapy has failed. It can also lower tension through the release of pent-up emotion, and stimulate the mind and memory.'

Among the many examples that illustrate the power of music, he cites a concert the two musicians gave at a hospice. One woman who had been admitted only three days before had been especially

Rachel Holt playing the flute for Live Music Now! at the Manchester Royal Infirmary.

unresponsive, and refused to attend the concert. Afterwards the two musicians played to some patients sitting out on the lawn. 'One of them asked if we could sing an Israeli song, and we complied with "Hava Nagila". We were only a few seconds into the song when a door on to the garden burst open, and out whirled a woman in dressing gown and slippers, clapping, dancing, and singing the song. She spent a long time talking to us afterwards, telling us about herself, and her particular love of songs. It was only later that we were told that she was the same "withdrawn" woman. The staff were flabbergasted at her reaction, as nothing and no one had been able to get through to her. After that she apparently settled in remarkably well.' (4)

Experience has shown that musicians involved in this kind of work need to have particular qualities in addition to a certain level of musical ability. Probably the most essential is the ability to communicate, both during the performance and in any session with patients afterwards. Increasingly the musicians are being encouraged to play on the wards, or even to individual patients in their rooms. Here the ability to use a lot of eye contact, to be prepared to hold a patient's hand while singing a song, are all necessary, as is a wide repertoire to meet patients' requests. Sylvia Lindsay stresses that the Council selects the musicians with care: 'When artists come to audition for us we know that if they fix their eyes on the floor or peer at us from behind a

music stand, they will not be right for the job,' she explains. (5) Nella Kerr has a similar policy: 'We look for warm, outgoing personalities, people who can communicate well with patients. It's important in these concerts that they make contact with the patients and move round amongst them.' (6)

The musicians need also to be able to show flexibility in what can often be very trying circumstances, where all kinds of interruptions can occur. Ian Edwards recalls some of the disturbances he has had to face: 'During the concerts you can get staff and visitors chatting, doctors visiting, the pill round, the library round, the tea round, visits by the chaplain, telephones ringing, the lift pinging, noise from the tea or coffee bar. It is rarely the patients themselves that are a problem.'(7)

Nevertheless, there can be interruptions from the audience, which the musicians need to have the resilience and sensitivity to handle. This kind of situation makes the occasion a very different one from a conventional concert performance, and can be at first very testing for the younger or less experienced performer. Even the more experienced need to be constantly on their mettle. Singer Ian Wallace recalls his first concert in Broadmoor, a special hospital for mentally ill patients. 'At one point one of the patients called out, "Mr Wallace, I want to do a number." I hastily whispered to the accompanist to let him have his request - though I was a bit nervous about his choice of "Frankie and Johnny". Afterwards he was quietly led away.' (8)

Many opera companies and orchestras now have a commitment to sending groups of singers or players out into hospitals and other health care institutions. The Royal Opera House, the London Mozart Players, the Scottish Chamber Orchestra and English Touring Opera are among the organisations now doing this. Another body that has organised a great number of such visits is Live Music Now!, set up in 1977 by Sir Yehudi Menuhin to provide opportunities for young musicians to play in a variety of community settings. Around a quarter of the thousand performances it arranges annually are in hospitals and hospices. Again, care is taken in the selection of performers, of whom there are currently more than 200 on Live Music Now!'s books, comprising around 75 groups.

There is an emphasis in auditions on finding friendly and lively personalities, with the right personal touch and informality to make the concerts as enjoyable and meaningful for the patients as possible, and to actively encourage participation. Many of the groups specialise in ethnic music from different countries; others may offer anything from reggae to string quartets.

Many of these concerts positively encourage patient participation, which may vary from making a request for an item to actually singing a favourite song. But as more general arts programmes come to be established in hospitals and elsewhere, many patients are being offered the opportunity to make music themselves, either as part of a group, or in one-to-one sessions.

In some places, such as Aycliffe Hospital in Darlington, a long-stay hospital for people with learning difficulties, they have been helped by a musician-in-residence. Katherine Norman, who held such a post there for a year in the mid-1980s, believes that only a full residency can begin to satisfy the patients' thirst for arts experience: 'For such residents, self-expression through art or music is a vital necessity; short-term residencies are not enough. The residents who worked with me on a regular basis, either in groups or one-to-one sessions,

expressed great enthusiasm. In fact, many of them demanded, and should have had, far more access to musical resources than I was able to offer.' (9)

Even without a musician-in-residence, regular musical opportunities are certainly easier to provide where there is an arts coordinator with a budget, who can liaise from the inside with individual ward sisters, therapists or day-care centre administrators about what patients may need. Gwyneth Lamb runs an arts programme at Earl's House Hospital in Durham, which also covers four other hospitals in the area. Here visiting musicians provide weekly music workshops, a combined music and dance group, a 'wandering minstrel', and a weekly participatory music session which has produced everything from tone poems to rock and roll. In the summer of 1991 there was a world music project, giving both residents and staff the opportunity to hear music of other cultures.

Gwyneth Lamb believes that the performing arts can play as important a part as the visual arts within a hospital: 'Of all the art-forms, music is perhaps the most emotionally evocative,' she suggests. 'It provides an intense individual experience and, at the

Below and next page 'Of all art-forms, music is perhaps the most emotionally evocative' : residents of Earl's House Hospital, Durham, work with the Durham Street Band.

same time, a very sociable activity.' She has found that it can offer 'an easy way in for both patients and staff who might be alienated by the idea of "the arts", but who might be comfortable listening to a singer or musician and find it easy to move from being an observer, on the outside looking in, to taking part on a simple level, singing along, swaying to the rhythm. From these simple beginnings much can develop.' (10)

Using the body

Like music, dance and movement can have an immediate effect on patients. Again, a mixture of performances by visiting professionals and projects which draw patients in to participate can be found all around the UK.

repertoire. The initial workout is often used to encourage participation by patients, who get a chance afterwards to talk to and question the dancers. Inger Newcomb, the ROH's administrator for this scheme, says that patients who have never seen ballet before are fascinated by what they are shown. 'The performances can give them a lasting impression of beauty and peace,' she says. 'The visits can also help to relieve the monotony of the daily routine.' (11)

Communication is a key element in such contact between artists and patients. One company that puts special emphasis on this is Common Ground Sign Dance Theatre, a full-time touring company which integrates disabled and able-bodied performers. In their work with children in hospital, for example, the

The Royal Ballet warming up at City Hospital, Nottingham, and in performance at the Northern Ireland Hospice, Belfast.

Since 1985, as part of its wider education programme, the Royal Opera House has been running its 'Invitation to the Ballet' scheme, in which dancers from the Royal Ballet at Covent Garden or the Birmingham Royal Ballet visit hospitals, hospices and day centres. The project was at first aimed at cancer patients, but more recently has extended into other areas, such as psychogeriatrics. The usual format is for the two dancers and a choreographer to demonstrate warm-up exercises, points of technique and different steps, before ending with a performance of items from the

company may find the need with one group to explain their work in English, Punjabi and British Sign Language. Here the aim before any performance is to engage all children in activity, even if they are confined to a hospital bed.

Encouraging patients to develop their own movement skills can be a way of developing their self-confidence, powers of self-expression and communication, and trust in others - all of which can be beneficial to their well-being or recovery. It can also bring out energy that seems to have been lost.

A Ludus Dance Company workshop with patients at The Empress, a residential home in Morecambe, Lancashire.

This is how one teacher working for Ludus Dance Company reported on her first term working alongside an elderly psychiatric group of patients, whom she met once a week for an hour:

'Inactivity becomes a habit, a habit difficult to overcome. In order to motivate the group, movement must bring pleasure rather than discomfort. I use movements that will promote feelings of safety and well-being, and will feed in a positive self-image. I hope to encourage them to discover their own limits and their full movement range. I am continually amazed at the sheer physicality of some of the clients. Those who looked so frail at first - S in her chair, B with her delicate mannerisms - have strength and flexibility in abundance when they choose to use it. Some, like F, are inclined to give up easily before they have even tried to do something, so it is essential to work through the resistance with patience and encouragement, and to take delight visibly in their achievements, no matter how small.' (12)

Achieving such aims requires sustained work on a regular basis over a period of time. During 1991/92 two movement teachers, Paul Wolf and Nikki Thomson-Stuart, spent several weeks working with people with learning difficulties at Borocourt Hospital near Reading. It was a challenging task: the hospital was in the last stages of a closure

programme, and some of the patients had been sectioned under the Mental Health Act, and so were prone to violent behaviour. The two workers used exercises and activities involving the body, which were designed to encourage group awareness and contact with others. The sessions concluded with a short presentation to other residents and members of staff. The two workers also held similar workshops with the staff, with the aim of passing on skills that they could subsequently use with the residents. The project, set up by Southern Artlink, encountered many practical difficulties, but appeared to bring benefits to the residents: the work was very different from anything normally available to them, it stimulated many who were normally withdrawn, and helped their social and group skills. Significantly, most of the staff felt the work to be a success, and there was a high attendance at the in-service training sessions. (13)

Training health care staff

Working with staff is increasingly seen to be a vital component in this kind of work, not just in order to pass on skills to be used with patients, but also to provide a change in routine or stimulation to staff working in difficult conditions.

Richard Coaten, an experienced dance teacher in the north of England, says that staff looking after elderly people feel the work has improved the quality of

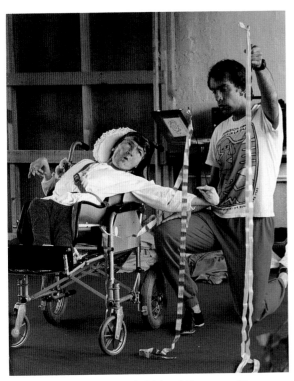

'Positive and life-affirming': Richard Coaten working on movement with a patient.

their lives: 'They say it develops their self-confidence and gives them more patience in working in small groups. They also find they have more ability to motivate the elderly people. They enjoy their work more because their clients do too, and it raises their morale because it is something positive, supportive and life-affirming for their patients.' (14)

Jabadao, a dance resource organisation based in Bradford, has worked for some years with the occupational therapy staff at Fieldhead Hospital in Wakefield, to promote self-awareness and enjoyment of dance and movement amongst patients with severe learning difficulties. The staff have picked up skills to a sufficiently high level that they are now in demand to provide advice and training to colleagues in other areas. The work is essentially non-verbal - the sessions are deliberately held in silence - and use is made of a variety of props, ranging from a parachute to streamers and masks. Jabadao's Penny Greenland says the training they have provided has helped staff a great deal: 'It's changed the way they relate as a team, they open up to each other in a different way. It's about building

up a relationship through the senses, so it gives them an opportunity to use their empathetic and intuitive side, instead of just thinking, as they normally do.' She stresses that the occupational therapy staff have developed a pride in their work, and that it has also helped them to endure the bleak and desolate environment of the hospital. (15)

Staff training is not only available in the dance and movement field. The organisation Community Music works with occupational therapists and nurses to show them how music can be best used with their patients. More and more nurses are going on general arts courses such as those run at St Joseph's Hospital in Rosewell, near Edinburgh. The nurses, the majority working with people with learning difficulties, initially experiment with several art-forms, and then begin to specialise in one, picking up the skills needed to be able to work with their patients. One of the early outcomes has been that nurses are beginning to see their patients more as individuals, and less as objects.

The performing arts are also beginning to make an appearance in formal nurse education. One of the pioneers here is the In Two Minds theatre project, set up in 1986 by nurse and drama therapist Jan Addison and Peter Watkins, nurse tutor at Suffolk and Great Yarmouth College of Nursing. 'We draw on drama therapy, psychodrama, theatre workshop, story-telling and performance drama,' Peter Watkins says. They try to help nurses to explore their emotional reactions to incidents in their work and to empathise more with their patients. 'Drama in therapy helps people face the drama of their lives, the challenge of change and misadventure, and to find a way forward. It's an holistic approach in which we try to focus on the affective side of health care.' (16)

Theatre and drama

Many nurses will already be familiar with drama in their own institution, since there are now several theatre companies and groups who include visits to hospitals, hospices and day centres as part of their community work. Forest Forge in the south of England, Word and Action from Dorset, the Geese Theatre Company in Birmingham, the Proper Job Theatre Company in Huddersfield, and the

Yorkshire Women Theatre based in Leeds are among the groups that bring productions and workshops into these places.

One of the more established companies in this field is Bedside Manners. A small-scale company set up in 1981 to bring musical theatre into hospitals and homes for long-stay patients and residents over 60, it has now expanded to include day-care patients and those in hospitals for the mentally ill. Their shows generally last around an hour, always include at least one audience participation number, and use a lot of eye contact with the audience. Artistic director Marie Macneill aims to dispel the idea that because they are performing to a 'minority' group, it doesn't matter if the standard is fifth rate. 'We place strong emphasis on the performers' ability to communicate in an upfront, unpatronising manner, and their ability to dance and sing at the highest professional level. This audience is as entitled as other members of the public to receive only the best, and not be treated as a professional stopgap.' (17)

Many of the company's shows are based on stories set in the past, and staff are encouraged to use the performances as a springboard for reminiscence. This is also the territory of Age Exchange, originally founded as a theatre company. Among its many reminiscence activities, Age Exchange mounts four or five productions a year, which use professional actors and are toured to a variety of venues, including hospitals. The plays explore social history themes - one recently focused on the NHS - using real experiences and memories. Older people whose lives are used for the material are sometimes themselves involved in developing the script and directing scenes drawn from their lives.

Most theatre companies can see the social and intellectual benefits of such reminiscence work. Paul Sneddon of Living Memory Theatre, the only professional company in the north of England which caters exclusively for elderly audiences, believes these can be considerable: 'The work is often a stimulus to long-term memory. It also enables people to establish their own identity, which has often been taken away from them. In care you feel less important, especially if you've just lost your home or your partner. The work helps to establish you, who

you used to be - and still are. It's also a very good way of people getting to know each other; they feel they have some common ground.' (18)

Other groups have noticed that theatre work in these settings can lift people out of their prescribed roles. Alison Whitworth and Penny Vowles, of Prism Theatre in Cumbria, believe one of the most significant consequences of the work is the way it changes staff perceptions of their patients. 'Having a space, in the usual, often hurried routine, to work together as equals on a project, or just to have the time "to be" and get to know someone on other terms, has a radical, positive impact on relationships. The sessions also provide a valuable opportunity for staff and carers to observe aspects of their clients they may not have noticed before.' (19)

As with music and dance, the subsidised national companies play their part in bringing in high-quality performances to health care institutions. Undoubtedly one of the most potent of such visits was when the Royal National Theatre Company took Deborah Warner's production of *King Lear* into the special hospital at Broadmoor early in 1991.

Three-quarters of Broadmoor's 500 patients are categorised as psychotic, the rest as psychopaths. Confronting such an audience was both challenging and disturbing: the company were acting out Shakespeare's brutal and violent tragedy in front of men and women who had themselves committed crimes of the utmost violence. After the performance the patients talked of their feelings about the play, showing in many cases how directly they related to the emotions being played out on the stage. The actors were later told by the consultant psychiatrist that the patients would probably be talking about the performance for months, perhaps years, and that they would come up in dreams and therapy sessions. She also told them that three patients, all of whom had killed one of their parents, had told her quite separately after the performance that they wished they could have been reunited with their parent in the way Cordelia was. (20)

There can rarely have been a more striking example of the power of the performing arts to play a part in the healing process.

A moment from Forest Forge's production, 'Bicycle Clips', which was toured to residential homes and day centres for elderly people.

Brian Cox's King Lear, with Cordelia (Eve Matheson): Broadmoor patients were greatly moved by the reunion of father and daughter.

Chapter 6
Writing and Reminiscence

If you can articulate pain
You're not overborne by it.
That is poetry's healing power.

- P J Kavanagh

While it's now quite common in Britain to find visual and performing artists working in hospitals and other places where health care is being provided, writers are much less in evidence. Only in the last five years has their potential in this field begun to be recognised, and a few enlightened authorities taken the step of employing writers-in-residence to work with patients, in one or more institutions.

Writing is about communication; the experience of being a patient, especially in hospitals, is all too often one of isolation. In one sense it is the simplest of all art-forms in which to involve patients. We all use words as part of our ordinary daily lives, and most people are capable of writing in some form or other - or, if prevented from doing so for some reason, of dictating words to another person for them to write down. In hospitals and hospices, writing can be a way of expressing feelings that may not otherwise have an outlet. It also provides a chance to reflect on the past, a subject to which so many people turn when their normal life is interrupted or changed by illness. It is here that the work of writers begins to overlap with or complement that of those engaged in reminiscence work, another growth area in recent years.

Writers-in-residence

Fiona Sampson is one of the more experienced writers in the health care field. As a poet she has worked on short-term residencies in a general hospital, a psychiatric hospital, long-stay elderly care units, and a psychiatric prison. During 1989/90 she took part in an ambitious pilot project, spending three days a week for 18 months as writer-in-residence for the entire Isle of Wight Health Authority. The residency was established to find out whether the benefits which patients around the country had clearly derived from being involved in art, craft, music and dance, might also apply to writing. The scheme was the first to use a writer in different areas of care in one authority: her brief was to work with children, acutely ill adults, long-term psychogeriatric and mentally infirm patients, people with severe learning difficulties, and hospice patients.

Looking back at her work, Fiona Sampson identifies her clients as having one thing in common: their vulnerability. 'This vulnerability sets patients apart from other groups; so much so that we can call it a special need. It's a need to explore - the situation, what they think and feel. It's a need to be individually accompanied through the experience. Often it's a need to have their own human dignity reasserted. Hospital staff, if they're not rushed off their feet, can help with this. So can a trustworthy outsider. But all this is rather patronising to the patient; and it seems to make a writer, in particular, redundant. The practice of writing, though, is more than this. In writing and dictated writing, the particular neediness is transformed into the important and universal: something other people can read, a work of art. Instead of a victim, we have someone with status: the patient is a writer.' (1)

For much of her residency she worked individually with patients, for around half an hour each. Her method was to encourage them to talk about something important to them, which would become the basis of their poem, story or description. If this proved difficult, she would pick out a theme from their general conversation, or read a couple of extracts from a poetry anthology. Often this was enough to persuade a patient to feel secure enough to write something of their own. In many cases, of course, patients were either physically unable to write, or the effort involved was too great for them. Here dictation, which is both informal and less tiring than writing, proved an effective way of enabling these patients to produce work of their own.

At other times, especially with patients with acute mental illness, she worked with small groups. All three of the island's day-care units hold discussion and trust groups, so it was relatively easy for the writing to be built into the programme, as another way to encourage participants to explore the feelings and thoughts that are part of their illness. Fiona Sampson's aim was to get them to try hard to be honest and understand themselves. She would lead the sessions by choosing a theme, and reading out extracts to illustrate it. After discussion, group members would write, and then read out what they had written. In this way they were able to share thoughts that many might not have been willing or able to admit to in a normal discussion group.

Her residency, which took her to 11 different buildings around the island, provoked some original and often moving work from patients who, in many instances, had never written anything personal before. Several were able to express violent emotions through the medium of poetry - such as one woman who had suffered two major heart attacks, and who began her poem:

You bastard you envy me.
What do I have that causes you such pain
The pain that generates your need to deflower me
depower me and put me down?

One woman who dictated a lyrical account of a childhood holiday in Dorset had said at the start of her session: 'Poetry? Not my kind of thing, love.' At the end she remarked: 'I didn't know I could write poetry.'

Fiona Sampson believes that part of a writer's effectiveness in these situations is due to not being seen as part of the health care staff. 'She's a fresh face and personality, but she's also able to act as an equal with clients. Her lack of a uniform makes her less threatening, and more able to establish a "normal" relationship with the client; this is an encounter, they feel, they could have had outside hospital. As a result, many patients who are rather afraid to express worries (or even complaints) to regular nursing staff, feel free to do so in writing sessions.' (2)

A writer clearly needs to have particular qualities in order to gain the trust of patients, who may be initially nervous, suspicious or simply uninterested. One of these is adaptability, the capacity to be flexible about the kind of writing to be produced, to be a facilitator rather than a teacher or critic. Lynne Alexander found this out at the very beginning of her year-long residency at Sobell House Day Centre in Oxford, where she worked with several patients who were in the last months of their lives:

'My first encounter was with Lynn, who had motor neurone disease. I had never met anyone with MND before, and I was thrown by her multiple incapacities, and the intelligence and frustration in her eyes. It was also a challenge to speak with her through the machine; I tried to read her body signals. But in spite of the difficulties and the paraphernalia of machinery between us, we built up some kind of

trust. She was a tough lady and I knew she wanted me to be honest with her, so I was. Maybe too honest. She began to admit her fears. She wanted to write the story of her illness, but she was rather obsessed with facts - getting it right. For a time I tried to get her to be more imaginative, in a sense to fictionalise her own experience. But that wasn't what she wanted, so I stopped that. It was my job to help her get it right according to her own light.'

This was not the only difficulty she met during the year. At first she was uncertain whether her work had anything to do with the healing of patients. After all, what use was writing? But soon she realised that it was precisely this 'uselessness' that was so valuable: because she was outside the medical system, people felt free to tell her things they would tell no one else. She also questioned the ethics of what she was doing. For a while she suppressed her own creative work, believing it would be voyeuristic to write about the patients. Eventually a joint poetry writing session made her change her mind: 'I discovered that it was not only okay for me to write, but necessary. After all, I was the writer and role model. So after that I allowed myself to write poems not only with patients, but for them, and this became part of the barter of mutual recognition through writing. The high point of this was the day I brought a poem for Christine, and found she'd written one for me too.'

She realised that writing was something people were not used to doing, and that it could be quite threatening at first. But over the year, she feels that both staff and patients came to accept her and take her seriously, and to realise that writing could be fun as well as challenging. Her work also proved directly beneficial to the staff's understanding of some patients. Examples of their writing were displayed on a board at the front entrance of the centre, and the social worker and medical director included some of the poems in their case notes, realising that the patients' work told them things their own examinations could not. As one patient put it: 'There are people at Sobell who look after our body, and Lynne looks after our mind.' (3)

The public display of patients' writings produced a similar effect at the new Springhill Hospice in

Rochdale, where writer Chrissie Gittins spent three days a week for six months in 1990/91 working with the 20 in-patients. With their permission she put their work up on a board in the corridor approaching the ward, where it could be easily seen by the staff. One staff nurse, Ann Howson, found this especially valuable: 'When I saw the board, I looked at my patients in a totally different way. They wouldn't have bothered to tell the nurses some of their feelings. But now we could say, "I've read what you said to Chrissie, and now I can help".'

The writing at Springhill had other uses too. One piece was read out at a patient's funeral; others were sent to friends and relatives. A selection of the work of both patients and staff was published under the title *Somebody Said That Word: Living in a Hospice*. Chrissie Gittins feels that the publication will help to allay the fears and prejudices people have about the quality of life in a hospice, as well as show how 'creativity can play a part in that quality'. (4)

But is it reasonable for writing of this kind to be shown to a wider public? Not all writers feel it is. One of these is Chris Hawes, writer-in-residence at Dove House Hospice in Hull. He has been taping and transcribing patients' life stories, and then revising them under their instruction. He makes two bound copies, with illustrations, one for himself, and one for the writer; further copies can be made for relatives and friends. He sees the work as allowing the patients to communicate with the next generation, but feels that commercial publication would be inappropriate, and possibly divisive. 'The writing is done for personal reasons, and under a promise of confidentiality,' he says. 'Patients owned the work themselves, and had total control. It wouldn't be fair to publish one person and not another; and to publish everything would be inconsiderate to the reader.'

This question of trust is central to the relationship between the writer and patients. Chris Hawes suggests that with such intimate and confessional work, the writer needs to be seen as completely trustworthy. He recalls one incident at Dove House that showed how such trust can pay off: 'I was talking to the husband of a patient who was expected to die shortly. He said he could tell me a story or

two, about himself, and when I encouraged him, he said "You won't tell anyone else?" I assured him I wouldn't. The husband then talked to his wife and the next day she wrote five poems, clear and cool messages for people close to her. You become a catalyst for things like that.' (5)

Some forms of writing are for a very specific audience. At Milestone House in Edinburgh, one of writer Andy Mackie's many tasks is to encourage some of the residents to write for their children. Milestone is a purpose-built facility in the grounds of the Edinburgh Royal Infirmary, providing hospice and respite care for 20 people with AIDS. It has an arts programme run by a full-time arts coordinator, which enables residents to take part in a range of activities, including art, video, stained glass and jewellery-making - and writing.

For two afternoons a week Andy Mackie is available to run writing workshops, or to work with individuals in their own room. Recently he advertised his services in the house's newsletter: 'You may not be around when your young son or daughter is old enough to understand things you'd like to say. In the future they may want to ask questions about you, but they'll only be able to hear the answers from other people. If you'd like to write something that they can read for themselves in the future, then see me privately, and I'll write it with you. All you have to do is tell me what you want to say.' Several parents have made use of this service. The writer's presence has encouraged two residents to work on a book and a play about their lives. It has also given some secret writers the chance to 'come out'. One result of this was the reading of a poem by a member of staff at a memorial service for one of the residents. (6)

A common feature of these and other projects is the way in which people of all ages and backgrounds, who have never written before, or have had bad experiences of writing at school, have been able to find their voice, and a new self-confidence as a result. Alison Kennedy, writer-in-residence for the Hamilton and East Kilbride District of Scotland in 1990, explains why contact in this situation between writer and patient can so often be fruitful: 'It's about letting people say what they don't even know they wanted to say,' she suggests. 'It's about your dreams, it's about your hopes, it's about how you feel about you, it's about the wee things you have little fantasies about, that keep you happy or keep you going, and communicating them to other people. And instead of getting red pen on them, or somebody saying you're daft, you get somebody saying, "Well, I found that interesting".'

Her work was with groups who came into contact with the Strathclyde social work department, including adults with learning difficulties attending day centres. Some were unable to speak, and had picture boards or touch talkers. She found that the unusual experiences of these adults, and the fact that they often had no outlet for their feelings, could lead to their imaginations running riot: 'The sentences and stories that come out are outrageous,' she says. 'And I mean, what were they doing before touch talkers were invented? For 20, 30, 40 years back? What was the deaf woman, who was not getting enough stimulus to want to turn her hearing aid on, doing for the 50 years before she started writing about what she saw on television, and how she didn't like Mr Gorbachev because she didn't trust him?' (7)

Remembering the past

Writing, even if done by means of dictation, does not suit everyone, as some of the professionals gradually realised. About halfway through her residency at Sobell House, Lynne Alexander found another means of encouraging residents to open up. 'I'm not quite sure how it happened,' she recalls, 'but one day I thought, let's try something new. So I got some patients together into a circle in the dining-room, and we began. I told a rather arcane American Indian story, but it didn't matter, because in no time they were off on subjects that interested them, from teddies to wartime evacuations to sexual mores. It was a revelation: this was what was missing, the chance to share memories and experiences. The sessions really caught on. Everyone has a story - many stories - to tell. If some of them get written down, so much the better. If not, it doesn't matter: it's the sharing of experience that counts, the opening up of minds and imaginations.' (8)

Such activity, based on encouraging elderly people to engage in story-telling and reminiscence, is no longer uncommon in hospitals, day centres and residential homes around Britain. Nor does it necessarily depend on having a writer-in-residence. The Reminiscence Project in Manchester, for example, has been using a variety of art-forms and artists in its work with elderly people since 1985. The project is based in Ladywell Hospital, Salford, and Winwick Psychiatric Hospital, Warrington, but also works in homes and day-care centres in the Manchester area. Activities vary, from a small tea-party to a music-hall evening, in which both patients and staff take an active part.

A recent fashion show at Ladywell shows the kind of collaboration the project aims for. The patients advised the staff about clothes of different periods, the staff made or found the clothes, the patients made fabric pictures of the fashions, and the staff acted as models for the show itself. Music of the period was also included. The idea grew out of a reminiscence session, and came from the staff rather than the project team.

'It was almost the perfect project,' says Roger Sim, the project's coordinator. 'We try to work towards a particular event, to give the activity meaning, rather than just dose the old people with the arts. The actual reminiscing is not the main thing: we're trying to create a context where there's more creative and expressive activity for old people; so we use any means to get that. It doesn't mean you don't value the art, it's just not the be-all and end-all: the creation of the piece of work is the excuse for activity. It also means that for a while the roles are reversed, and the patients are the experts. It's about having someone around who looks at the strengths of patients, whereas the nurses, when someone is comfortable, they go and look for someone who isn't - that's their job.'

The project sets special store on working closely with staff - indeed, Roger Sim says that in many respects staff are the project's clients more than the patients. 'In the old days the staff had no role: therapists did therapy, nurses did nursing,' he says. He and his colleagues now use nursing auxiliary staff as 'link workers', who negotiate free time to work with the project, and help to set up the arts and reminiscence events and programmes. The project

Top and left
*Reminiscence work at
Withington Hospital,
Manchester.*
Below *Ladywell
Hospital, Salford.*

offers them ideas, support and practical help, including a collection of memorabilia for the reminiscence sessions.

Roger Sim believes that the work at Ladywell Hospital has changed the culture of some of the wards. In place of the formerly drab walls and curtains and old lockers, there are now pictures, stained-glass windows, china instead of plastic cups, and new colour schemes for curtains and cushions

chosen by the patients. The hospital used to be known locally as 'the place you waited to die', but attitudes have changed. He suggests that relations between staff and patients have changed too: 'They're more respectful of patients, they've started to realise people notice little aspects of their behaviour.' Some link workers say the whole feeling

Tea and sympathy: dancer and resident during Hospital Arts' tea-dance at a residential home, Manchester.

of the place has changed. Where previously patients used to sit and stare at the walls for most of the day, now they know each other's first names, and talk to each other. One suggested that the project had changed her whole view of the job, and that she now saw the patients as her friends.

Inevitably, the project has met resistance, as Roger Sim explains: 'Staff don't always participate as much as we'd like - through fear, lack of confidence, or shortage of time. And for all those who are keen, there are just as many who think it's not their role, or who say, "Our people won't respond to that, they just want a sing-song." We try to prove them wrong. But you can only offer opportunities; you can't force them to do it.' (9)

Being based in a hospital clearly has many advantages. For the individual writer coming into a strange institution, it can be very difficult to effect any change to accepted routines, as Lynne Alexander remembers: 'It's difficult for someone in my position to go against that grain of well-established, comfortable and comforting routines, and to whip up enthusiasm for something new and strange-seeming and perhaps intimidating. At times I felt I had to fight for space, both literally and figuratively: I had to prove creative writing's worth and my own, in an atmosphere devoted not to the encouragement of real openness and creativity, but to keeping patients busy and cheerful. I got a feeling of "This is how we do things here: we sew wallets, we play cards, we cut and paste greetings cards, we drink tea and eat cakes and play word games. We keep things moving: drinks at 11, lunch at 12, tea at 4; men to the left, women to the right." I can remember screwing myself up to do my first group writing session, and being told by one of the volunteers, "Oh no, today's our word-game day." I felt like an intruder, and went away.' (10)

There may also be conflicting views of what such a residency can achieve, and of what the priorities should be. Chrissie Gittins met with this sort of problem at Springhill. 'There were differences in expectation over the content of the end-product of the residency,' she remembers. 'Being a charity without NHS funding, the hospice management were anxious to promote public relations. I was more

concerned with the creativity of the patients. The fundraising officer tried to take over the project at the beginning, and that made for a very difficult relationship.' (11)

No one should underestimate the stress and the isolation that writers can experience in such work, however rewarding and challenging it may be. Probably only a minority of writers would be able to work effectively in such a setting. Yet those who have attempted to work in this way certainly feel that the experience has enriched their own writing - and not just because it has given them fresh material to work on.

Ultimately of course, both writing and reminiscence work have to be judged according to the benefits that they bring to patients. Fiona Sampson is convinced that her Isle of Wight residency has not just been a diversion, but has had beneficial therapeutic effects. 'This makes a clear case for access to writing as a regular part of high-quality patient care. Every nurse knows that a sustained personal relationship with the patient is part of good practice. The writing project simply takes this art of talking and listening one step further. Anything which benefits patients to such a degree that, as members of the team have noted, they stop needing NHS care sooner than they might otherwise have done, is valuable.' (12)

But is it Medicine?

Withymoor Surgery Arts
Project, Brierley Hill, Dudley,
West Midlands

'We have seen people grow in confidence, have more patience with their children, make friends and overcome grief, all because of the therapeutic arts in the surgery. One patient said she thought she'd "died and gone to Heaven" when she walked into the waiting room.'

New patients coming into Dr Malcolm Rigler's Withymoor village surgery in Brierley Hill might be forgiven for registering surprise at their surroundings. Waiting rooms in doctors' surgeries and health centres tend to be dull, functional places, the only 'decoration' being a pile of magazines, or the odd notice or tattered poster warning you of the dire consequence of unhealthy habits or behaviour.

Malcolm Rigler's surgery is something different. The tables are covered with brightly patterned fabric. On the walls are a series of witty, colourful anti-smoking posters: one says, 'Lungs put air in your chest'; another asks, 'Do you pollute the tree in your trunk?' Other spaces are filled by equally jokey mobiles. In one corner is the 'lung box', made by local children, and showing by means of coloured objects how heavy smoking can affect your lungs.

But the difference is not just in the decor. In the last four years the surgery, situated in the middle of a row of shops in Withymoor, has become as much a community arts centre as a village surgery. There has been live music for mothers attending ante-natal classes; local theatre groups performing cabaret or educational work in the waiting room; a writer-in-residence working with people of all ages; and an art teacher from the local community school spending one day a week helping to develop patients' artistic abilities.

This welter of arts activities originated from Malcolm Rigler's conviction that his brief as a GP was not simply to diagnose illness and provide prescriptions, but to take some responsibility for the morale of the community. If the community is not functioning properly, he believes, then the people don't function properly either. His surgery serves a housing estate, built only 15 years ago for 11,000 people, and inhabited by property-owning families with young children. Most are factory workers in light industry or people with small businesses. There are some retired people, from widely differing social backgrounds: a few solicitors, accountants and teachers, but also unskilled and semi-skilled workers. The surgery has 3,500 people on its list, with 360 children under five.

Nurse practitioner Lynda Lawley, who has been with the practice for eight years, remembers her early days: 'Here in Withymoor there was no community. Mothers and their children spent hours on their own with nowhere to go; teenagers roamed the streets looking for something to do; men either worked so hard they were uptight and had no relaxation, or else they'd lost their job and were worried to death anyway. With so much redundancy and high mortgage rates, they were no better off than people living on a council estate.'

No useful play facilities were provided and there was no meeting place on the estate. With no obvious social network there was a lot of stress amongst patients coming to the surgery, especially young women isolated at home with their children. Malcolm Rigler felt that patients could not be treated in isolation from their environment. 'I came to realise that the diagnosis of a single complaint always involved an understanding and sometimes an intervention into the culture, stories and traditions of the neighbourhood.'

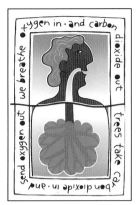

Above and pages 72-75
Posters (also printed as postcards) by John Angus and Alison Jones for the 'A Breath of Fresh Air' project at Withymoor.

His first move was to invite two artists, Alison Jones and Art Hewitt, to take up a week-long residency in the surgery. They taught story-telling to patients in the waiting room, and provided live music - suitably low-key so as not to disturb the work of the surgery. They also showed patients how to make greetings cards. The idea quickly attracted many young mothers, who welcomed the chance to take part in activities that enabled them to meet others. Soon it became standard practice for every woman on the Withymoor list to receive a hand-made congratulations card on the birth of their child.

The week had been a reconnaissance visit on behalf of Welfare State International, a collection of artists whose many skills include the visual arts, environmental design, music, story-telling, performance, pyrotechnic animation, and giant puppetry. The group suggested that the surgery might initiate a lantern procession as a way of celebrating the coming of spring, which at the same time would provide the focus for a much-needed community event. 'Local people weren't used to running anything,' Malcolm Rigler says.

'You make friends when you make lanterns' : 400 local people now join in the annual lantern procession in Withymoor.

To get it going, the artists met with small groups in the surgery waiting room, and showed them how to make decorated lanterns, which they then finished at home or school. When the procession was held in March 1990, some 20 families were represented. The following year - with the full support of the nearby Withymoor Primary School - 250 people came. By 1992 the number joining in was 400. Next year the event will include a firework display.

The celebration has clearly sparked off a considerable amount of community spirit, as well as established a tradition in a community that previously had none. 'It's a very special evening,' Lynda Lawley says. 'Everyone is singing and dancing and talking, and the magical glow of lanterns stretches as far as the eye can see. It may not sound much, but to make someone smile and forge a few friendships is better than any medicine. You make friends when you make lanterns.'

Another initiative brought in the local writer and poet Dave Reeves. His work entailed offering writing advice on anything from letter-writing to poetry, from reminiscence work to writing fiction. Malcolm Rigler's hope is that he will also be able to build up an oral history of the area, in particular information about the experiences of children and adults of illness and medical care. 'We've had some super poems from the children on their experience of medicine,' he remembers. 'We also got a lot of local history, all mixed up with folk remedies.' Apart from its intrinsic value, the writing on health topics is seen as being of direct medical use, since it enables both patients and staff to explore issues and anxieties in more depth than normal.

Malcolm Rigler's belief is that a writer should be employed in all districts to assemble such information from a community, so that the results can be put onto a database. He envisages a health care menu which for just a few pence would give you a computer printout of a story or poem that related to your illness, which you could then share with others. 'I would hope people would then find it perfectly acceptable to drop in and find out how others have coped with illness, without actually seeing the doctor.'

Another aim at Withymoor has been to make the surgery a place of fun and enjoyment for children. The staff discovered that 10% of parents were failing to bring their children in for their pre-school vaccination. So Lynda Lawley devised a scheme that turned what can often be a painful experience into a party, to which children received formal invitations. When they turned up, they found the waiting room transformed into a castle by students from Thorns Community School. An anaesthetic cream was applied to ease the pain of the jab, and the children were then given some painting work to do at home while the cream took effect. Lynda Lawley explains the next step: 'When they returned to the surgery two hours later, they were taught some simple percussion techniques by the students, they looked at each other's paintings, and played in the castle. They also of course had their injection. At the end none of them wanted to go home.'

The latest idea is to have a story-teller in the surgery, inviting patients to tell him about the problems that have brought them there. The stories are then told to groups of children and invited audiences in the waiting room. 'It's been compelling, and a fruitful avenue of communication,' Malcolm Rigler says. 'Most of the patients don't read books, but they do listen to stories. The life of a person is a story, and an artist can make all the difference, they can get them to understand the importance of their own lives by saying, "This is the truth as I see it, can I share it with you?"'

All this activity, so closely akin to community work, has attracted some criticism from other health professionals. They suggest the medical needs of Withymoor people are being neglected, or that activities such as the lantern procession

'The life of a person is a story, and artists can make all the difference': Malcolm Rigler in his surgery.

stretch the definition of nursing too far. The staff counter this by emphasising that 95% of their time is spent on conventional nursing and medicine, and that the arts activities constitute preventative medicine.

Within the community there has generally been enthusiastic support for the arts programme. Everyone has noticed the waiting room; many elderly people now say it's a pleasure to come to the doctor's. Instead of delaying a visit until they are really sick, many people have turned up simply in order to have a good time. A handful of patients has left the list, preferring a more traditional approach; but most like the changes. There have been minor misjudgements - such as when some of the live music played at an ante-natal clinic was criticised for being too intrusive. Malcolm Rigler, however, is quite convinced of the benefits. 'People's lives have changed. Some of us can see the arts having a dramatic effect, as strong as penicillin, on getting patients where they need to be. The artists have helped people to get better or, if they don't, to accept it like an adult, rather than a dependent child. It's also kept staff very buoyant and morale high; there's always a project to look forward to. It balances up having to cope with so much distress.'

In 1989, following her involvement with the Brierley Hill project, Alison Jones and other artists set up a new organisation, Celebratory Arts for Primary Health Care, with the aim of doing similar work in other practices. 'There is a great and growing demand for what we have to offer,' she says. 'Our positive vision strikes a chord with many health professionals.' They have set up workshops in other surgeries, followed by an exhibition in Gateshead of their work, which provoked a great many inquiries from doctors. A recent £10,000 grant from the King's Fund quality of life scheme has enabled them to spread their work further. They will be holding seminars for GPs on how to set up workshops in their surgeries, and involving elderly people in health centres and residential homes in Gateshead in arts activities, based on the theme of The Heart.

Such pioneering work brings its own difficulties where funding is concerned. 'We cross barriers, we're about bringing people together, so we don't fit into a convenient category,' Alison Jones explains. Malcolm Rigler recalls a slightly different obstacle: 'Arts funders initially argued that doctors don't have anything to do with the arts.' Such preconceptions were eventually overcome when people understood and saw what was going on at Withymoor. Since then West Midlands Arts, Dudley Council, Cadbury and other trusts have between them provided £20,000 worth of funding, including £7,000 secured from the Arts Council for the writing residency.

The Brierley Hill project will still be seen by many doctors as revolutionary, or inappropriate to patients' needs. Yet the idea of helping a community to promote its own health and well-being is one that many of those involved in its support see as important to the future of both the arts and general practice. David Hart, literature officer at West Midlands Arts, is one of those who applauds its radical aims and principles: 'Underlying all this work, the connection is being made between health and creativity, between well-being and self-empowerment, between community health and shared artistic endeavour.' With the help of community leaders, a Brierley Hill Arts Education and Health Group has been set up, to provide a support structure for the work.

Malcolm Rigler is encouraged by what has been done so far, but is keen to go even further. 'I see us expanding and making much more sophisticated the very notion of "information", as a creative exercising of the imagination, where fiction and poetry as well as straight description, letter-writing and diary-keeping happen, and, while respecting individual writing, to encourage as well a community basis for it.'

He also is sure that such 'nursing' of a community is the way forward for general practice. 'As doctors we can only care for people by looking at the whole, not just the sum of the parts,' he argues. 'Doctors of the future cannot practise at arm's length; it's no longer acceptable for us to sit back and wait for people to become ill. And if art is a way of educating the community about their health, that's what we must use. Most stress-related diseases are tied up with a lack of imagination and understanding; I feel big public-health issues can be approached by artists better than anyone else.'

· keep your lungs in tune ·

Chapter 7
Lessons from Practice

'We have to play down what we're doing. It's controversial; some people are not sure about money being spent on art.'

Arts coordinator for a Midlands hospital

It has taken time for arts projects to gain acceptance in the health care field. For many years there was resistance to such ideas, to anything out of the ordinary that might cause problems for the bureaucracy. Absurd arguments, such as 'Pictures attract dust and germs' or 'We don't want theatre groups coming in here with their clodhoppers on, shouting and swearing', were advanced in order to prevent change.

Now, however, the culture of the NHS is changing, and more and more managers are looking for creative ideas. This makes it even more necessary for arts projects to be planned, executed and evaluated professionally. Where this is done successfully, it becomes easier to break down the prejudices that still exist in some places about using the arts as part of health care.

Origins

You don't need to be a professional artist or a hospital manager to see the need for improving the health care environment and the quality of life for patients and staff. It's no surprise then to find that, while the practice of introducing the arts into health care has spread, the origins of the projects that have been set up over the last two decades have been many and varied.

The idea may have come from a consultant or GP, recognising that the arts can be an important part of the healing process. It may have originated from a nurse, who has realised that patients need a more comforting environment, or a chance to take part in creative activities. It may have come from other staff tired of walking down bleak and dismal corridors, or from patients fed up with sitting in an outpatient clinic or health centre staring at blank walls or reading the same posters over and over again. It may have been sparked off by a visiting relative, horrified at the forced inactivity of a member of their family, or the depressing conditions in which they are having to live. It may have arisen from the frustrations of a hospital manager, concerned about the incoherent jumble of fuse boxes, fire hydrants, arrows, lights, and the proliferation of handmade and other notices scattered throughout the building. Or it

may have emerged from the dissatisfaction over working conditions of a member of the works department in a hospital, of a cleaner, a porter, or a member of the kitchen or catering staff. Often all it has needed is for one person to see the need for change, and to want to do something to bring it about.

However, once the need has been identified, it is vital that the process becomes a partnership between all the parties involved. There's no doubt that the most successful projects have been those where consultation, discussion and negotiation with staff have been built into the project from the beginning, and where sensitive and realistic planning has been a feature. What then are the main considerations to be borne in mind at each stage?

Getting started

Most worthwhile projects have started with the formation of a representative group of people. A working arts committee or steering group of this kind is essential, not just so that different interests can be represented, but so the work can be shared, and different skills and expertise drawn on. The composition of the group is very important: it needs positive thinkers who are sympathetic to the arts, and enthusiastic about improving the quality of the health care environment. The group should comprise a good cross-section of people, but should also be as high-powered as possible. If, for example, it includes a senior medical person or administrator, it is more likely to gather support for its ideas, both from within and outside the health care community concerned.

Once such a committee is in place, a strategy will need to be drawn up, based on identifying specific needs and priorities. How this is done will depend on the scale and nature of the project. Many groups have commissioned an arts consultant or agency to advise them at this stage. Whatever the way forward, there is a need for a plan to be devised, covering aims and objectives, the budget, fund-raising, the timetable, commissioning, the role of the artist, monitoring and evaluation, promotion and publicity, and aftercare and maintenance. It is essential that every project continues to have a strong advisory group for the duration of its activities.

The arts coordinator

Experience has shown how important it is at an early stage to appoint one person to coordinate the work. With smaller projects this has sometimes been the part-time responsibility of an existing member of staff within the hospital, health centre or health authority. Increasingly, however, and certainly where a larger programme of arts activity has been envisaged, a full-time arts coordinator has been appointed. Once a coordinator is appointed, he or she needs to be sure of gaining the support of the steering group and the hospital management for all aspects of the arts programme.

Depending on the availability of funding, the coordinator is usually employed initially for a period of between six months and two years. The job normally requires someone with art training, who may be employed in the first instance to work on a particular commission. In other cases, they may be asked to coordinate existing arts activities, or to plan a programme from scratch, in consultation with the steering group. Once established, the coordinator may be appointed to the health authority staff.

Experience has shown that such a person is best placed to consider the needs of the community, to communicate on a regular basis with patients and staff, to understand their views and requirements, and to prevent the 'here today, gone tomorrow' approach which can rightly provoke criticism of projects undertaken without consultation or even explanation. But to do this successfully they need certain qualities - not least because, though there has been a great deal of progress, there is still a lot of work to do to convince some health care staff that the arts can be of benefit within their environment.

The arts coordinator can often be the key to the success or failure of the project. Ideally she or he should have the following qualities:

● A wide experience of the arts, combined with organisational skills.

● Vision, creative ideas, flair, and aesthetic sensibility.

● The ability to match artists, projects and people, recognising the suitability or otherwise of art-forms and arts activities for different health care settings.

● The flexibility to accommodate other people's ideas.

● The ability to communicate, explain and deal sensitively and diplomatically with people from all walks of life.

● Enough courage, tenacity and stamina to overcome ignorance, prejudice, disappointments and setbacks.

Funding

A programme of work can take many forms, and consist of one or more projects. The range of work described in the previous chapters gives some indication of the rich diversity of projects that have been established in recent years. Yet whether the project lasts a day, a week, a month, or two years, once practical details are established it will need to have an agreed budget.

It is then that the question of fund-raising has to be tackled. In general, most arts programmes are financed from several different sources, both inside and outside the health authority. The following are the most usual sources of funding:

● Regional Arts Boards. Previously called regional arts associations, their record so far is good, although it can depend rather too often on the enthusiasm and commitment of an individual officer. Although an application to a RAB can be time-consuming, the eventual sum granted can be substantial, and worth the effort. However, a RAB will rarely provide more than half of the money required.

● Arts and leisure departments in local authorities.

● Health authorities and trusts.

● Hospital trust funds. This is money endowed for the general well-being of patients, and as such is separate from the general clinical budgets.

● Organisations such as the Friends of the Hospital, or the local branch of the Women's Royal Voluntary Service, many of which run shops and canteens in hospitals.

● Charitable trusts and foundations. There are literally hundreds of these, so it is important to identify which of them are particularly interested in arts, health care or arts education or community projects. An up-to-date list and guidance on how to apply are to be found in *The Directory of Grant-Making Trusts* and other directories.

● Private or business donations. These may be from local firms, or families who have benefited from the health care provided. Such donations can also be in the form of materials or equipment.

● Corporate sponsorship. This again may be from a local firm, or from the local branch of a multi-national or national firm. As with trusts and foundations, competition for funds is fierce, so applications have to be carefully thought out, well-targeted, professionally presented, and made in good time.

● The Association for Business Sponsorship for the Arts. This government-run body administers a business sponsorship incentive scheme, which contributes money raised for the arts from business. These awards are made to arts organisations and businesses, so hospitals or health centres have to work in partnership with such a body from the beginning of a project.

● Payroll giving. Some hospitals and health centres now run this scheme for its employees to give to charities and other good causes.

Some projects have found other, less conventional ways of attracting funding. One hospital programme obtained money from the local tourist board, because it convinced the board that improvements to the hospital grounds would encourage visitors to its beautiful surroundings, where they could picnic and enjoy the relaxed atmosphere, or visit the collection of paintings within the hospital buildings. Another approached a water authority that had recently attracted adverse press publicity, and persuaded it to donate a 'water feature'. Help may also come in kind in the form of labour: in one hospital arts project young farmers helped with the landscaping, while in another a nature conservation group took responsibility for the exterior landscaping and grounds.

In the past the bulk of the fund-raising for arts in health care projects has been undertaken by the arts side of the partnership. Increasingly, however, the health side is coming to recognise the benefits of money raised for and invested in a good arts programme. It is to be hoped that they will now be able to take on more of the fund-raising than previously, so that a balance is struck. It has in any case become increasingly unlikely that external sources will offer funds unless they know that the health authority, hospital or health centre has contributed in one way or another, or that they will gradually take over the funding after an initial period. Here account needs to be taken of the variety of resources in kind which an institution can provide. Covering such items as accommodation, domestic services, cleaning, lighting, heating, secretarial and administrative services, transport or materials, these often add up to a substantial sum.

Projects are increasingly using a business plan as a key part of their efforts to raise funds. An attractive, clear and brief plan, outlining the aims and benefits of the project, will greatly enhance the chance of making a successful application. Such a plan should answer the following questions:

● What do you aim to do?

● Why are you doing it?

● Why is it needed?

● For whom is it intended?

● Is your idea an appropriate one?

● How long will it take to carry out?

● How much will it cost?

● Who will manage the project?

● Have you raised any funds towards it?

● How will it be monitored and evaluated?

Experience has shown that it also pays to have a leaflet or brochure which explains aims and objectives by including illustrations from existing successful projects. This, in conjunction with the business plan, can then be sent to potential funders, members of the health authority and the local community. Local companies are often very willing to put up the relatively small sum needed to cover the printing of such a brochure, and have their name associated with it.

Funding doesn't get any easier, and there is some evidence that the formation of health authority trusts is delaying the funding of arts projects. Nevertheless, more and more hospital managers are finding creative ways to fund worthwhile projects. It is not generally known or believed that a considerable amount of arts activity is now being paid for out of health authority funds. When, for example, someone in a hospital service retires or goes on maternity leave, a saving of a few thousand pounds is enough to start an arts project. This initial money then gives all involved time to apply for funds from other sources.

Briefing and selecting the artists

It is important from the outset to make clear to the artists or craftspeople what is expected of them. For performing groups, or individuals coming in for a one-off session, this is a relatively straightforward matter, and normally handled by the arts coordinator through prior discussion and a simple letter of contract. Where the project entails a more regular or long-term involvement - for example, through a residency, or a commission for a specific piece of artwork in the building - then a clear procedure is essential for all concerned.

Before an artist is selected for this kind of project, it is essential that a brief is prepared and agreed upon. It should obviously include all the basic details about fees, timetable, deadlines, organisation, and resources available. But it should also provide a clear indication of the precise kind of work that is required, the timescale for the project, the personal qualities being looked for, and, where relevant, how the artist might be expected to relate to patients and

staff. Errors and misunderstandings can all too easily arise if such matters are not spelt out as precisely as possible before the work begins.

Depending on the nature of the project, there are several different ways of finding the most suitable artist. At its simplest, it can be a straight commission from a known visual artist whose work appeals to the commissioners. A more common method of commissioning is to pay a small number of artists to prepare a design for a specific site, and to select one to be carried out. Where the aim is, say, to appoint an artist, musician or writer-in-residence, then the usual method is open competition, and the post is advertised regionally or nationally. The greater risk involved with this method is balanced by the wider choice, and the possibility of unearthing appropriate talent.

Consultation and communication

Working in a health care setting demands a sympathetic approach on the part of the artist, and an understanding of how the system works. It should never be forgotten that the work is intended to be primarily for the benefit of other people, and to be part of the healing process. It is vital therefore that the artist makes sure that the right people are consulted as the work progresses.

Take the case of an artist who has been commissioned to brighten up a particular area of a hospital building. They will want to start with discussions with the staff and other users of that area, to reach agreement on the overall effect to be achieved, the type of artwork that might be appropriate, and potential themes to be explored. A number of questions may arise at this stage: If murals are to be considered, when would the area be due for redecoration by the works department? Could the budget for this be contributed to the overall funding of the project? Will further funding be required? What is the likely timetable?

The artist will then prepare one or more designs, taking into account the views of the sisters, nurses, doctors, and ancillary workers who use the site. They will also consider the size and position of the existing floors, lights and colours, and whether the estates department needs to be approached to carry out any repairs. The next stage is to make a presentation to the staff and management of the alternative designs, and to reach agreement on the one to be carried out.

Once this has been secured, the artist will need to keep in regular contact with staff and patients, in order to maintain their interest and enthusiasm. Where the work is being done in a corridor or very open area, this is likely to happen as a matter of course as people pass by. If on the other hand it is being carried out in, say, an X-ray room or a similarly enclosed space, then more of an effort will be needed to keep in touch.

During the work it is important that good relations are established with the trade unions. In the past there have been misunderstandings and disputes over territory, some of which could have been avoided if proper communications had been established from the beginning. The works department in a hospital, for example, is responsible for decoration and the upkeep of walls, and would need to be involved in any decisions relating to the painting of murals or the hanging and positioning of works created elsewhere.

The artist will of course be working closely with the arts coordinator during this time. But it also makes sense for them now and then to report on progress to the arts committee, or at least to a group drawn from it, who can provide advice and encouragement as well as constructive comment. This kind of informal support system can be invaluable for helping the artist to discuss any problems that may arise, and to get a sense of how different people are reacting to the work.

Sharing the responsibility

Managers and artists need to work together if a project is to succeed. Without good management it will not be effective, may not last long, and have only a superficial effect.

While the artist is obviously responsible for the quality of the work of art, the overall management of the physical environment and the social organisation

in which the work is being carried out is the responsibility of the health authority, or the hospital or health centre manager. Since arts projects are increasingly being linked to the quality of health care, it can be useful in hospitals, for example, to bring them alongside the estates department, with the estates manager having the responsibility for them. In this situation, the arts coordinator is still in charge of the day-to-day running of the project, but is ultimately responsible to the appropriate senior manager.

Specific areas of responsibility for managers are contracts for artists and commissions; raising and managing the necessary finance; business planning for the project; developing a strategy for implementation; monitoring progress; organising publicity for the project; and ensuring that funders are given feedback. In practice, some of these functions can be shared with the arts coordinator.

Monitoring and evaluation

It is always a good idea to document the project as it goes along. This may be done by taking photographs at different stages of the work; by making a video film, which includes the reactions of a good cross-section of people involved; by the artist keeping a diary; or by a combination of all three methods. Such documentation can be useful in explaining and promoting the project to the various interested parties, including the local community. It can also prove immensely valuable when money needs to be raised for further projects.

It is also useful and important to establish whether the aims of the project, and the needs of those it is aimed at, are being met according to the original plan and brief. This will clearly involve seeking the opinions of a representative cross-section of staff, patients and others affected, as well as those of the artist. This should certainly be done at the end of the project, but if possible at an earlier stage too. Such an evaluation might be carried out by one or more of the arts committee, by the arts coordinator, or in some cases by an outside researcher. This last method may be preferable where the project appears to have got into difficulties, or where it is felt that an external, objective evaluation may be especially needed.

In carrying out this exercise, the underlying aim will be to try to assess how far the project has been beneficial to patients, either directly, or indirectly through its positive impact on staff. This is not a piece of scientific research, so the evidence will tend to be anecdotal, but still immensely useful.

Nevertheless, a report that looks critically at the outcome of the project through the eyes of a reasonable cross-section of people affected is likely to contain some valuable lessons, both for the immediate present and the future. In many cases, a worthwhile arts project can lead to the establishment of a long-term programme, and to the permanent employment of an arts worker or arts team. Such a programme is the most effective way of meeting the needs of the whole community. But without proper evaluation of the original project, it is unlikely to come about.

Promotion and publicity

Publicity can be gained in one or more of the following ways:

● By staging an official opening ceremony for any significant work of art, or the launch of an arts programme.

● By mounting an exhibition, using the documentation of the project. Here it is useful to show not just the final piece or pieces of artwork, but also the process which the project has gone through. For the visual arts, 'before and after' pictures are especially effective.

● By keeping the media in touch with the project, and giving journalists and reporters opportunities to provide coverage. This is particularly important in relation to local newspapers, radio and television. The arts coordinator is generally the person who deals with the media; otherwise one person needs to be appointed to do this important job - perhaps a member of the arts committee.

● By ensuring that the leaflet or brochure about the programme is widely circulated to key individuals and groups, including actual and potential funders, local community groups, members of the health authority, local schools, the Friends of the Hospital, the WRVS, and other voluntary bodies.

● By creating posters or postcards of any finished artwork, which not only provide a permanent record of the work, but generate income for future projects.

● By publishing the final evaluation report as a document for discussion - unless there are good reasons for not doing so, or for only publishing it in condensed form.

Although there has been an enormous increase in the use of the arts in health care, it is still very necessary to make a good case for the part they play. So there is a responsibility to promote and publicise good work: one project can create an opportunity for the next. Such publicity will be good for the hospital or health centre and its community. It is essential for the arts programme in order to gain potential support for future programmes.

All Across the Authority

Healing Arts: Isle of Wight

'The ingredients were all there: there was this keenness in everyone, a will to succeed, strong leadership, and no resistance. It was as if nothing was impossible.'

John Bird, commissioning and development manager for the new St Mary's Hospital in Newport, Isle of Wight, is recalling the time in the early 1980s when the building was still just a gleam in the planning team's eye. The concept was a bold one: to create a new hospital which, for the first time in the UK, involved an extensive plan for the arts as an integral part of its design for a healing environment. In September 1991 the dream became a reality, with the official opening of St Mary's.

Yet there is much more to the Isle of Wight initiative than just a new hospital building. The arts are also flourishing in other health care settings around the island - in existing hospitals, health centres, day centres and clinics. This is due in large measure to a decision in 1984 by the DHSS and the Isle of Wight Health Authority to commission a feasibility study for an arts project for the whole authority. The eventual result was the establishing of Healing Arts: Isle of Wight, coordinated by Guy Eades, who divides his time equally between providing an arts programme for St Mary's, and one for Community Health Services which is delivered throughout the island. It's a pioneering authority-wide service that offers an exciting model for other health authorities to consider.

At St Mary's itself, the contrast with the traditional hospital environment could hardly be more striking. Where so often there is drabness and monotony, here there is light and variety. In place of featureless and unending corridors, there are bright and attractive 'streets', with large windows giving views out on to plant-lined and pebbled internal courtyards. Artwork - designed to soothe, divert and inspire - is everywhere: in the outpatients area, in the consulting and X-ray rooms, on the children's ward, on the stairway walls and other public areas.

This achievement is due to the unique and sustained teamwork of Peter Senior, arts adviser to the hospital, the architect Richard Burton of Ahrends, Burton and Koralek, the interior designer Stephen Nicoll, John Bird and his commissioning team, and Guy Eades. Their underlying aim was to create a healing environment in which landscape, design, architecture and artwork were approached in a unified way, rather than treated separately and piecemeal.

Below and next page
St Mary's Hospital,
Isle of Wight.

As Guy Eades puts it: 'St Mary's marks a renaissance in the understanding of how the arts contribute to a building's efficiency, and its ability to achieve its principal objectives in health care.'

One of the most striking and original features of the new St Mary's is the use of the themes of water and landscape, reflecting the life of the island. You see this first, literally, in the large lake at one side of the building. Previously a small, silted-up pond that dated back to the original buildings of 1770, it is now an attractive wildlife area. The water, surrounded by shrubs, lawns and seats, with a small footbridge in the centre, provides a home for ducks, swans and goldfish. Based loosely on the design of Monet's

celebrated water garden at Giverny, it offers mobile patients a tranquil space in which to recuperate, and others a restful view through the windows of their wards.

The chosen themes are clearly visible indoors - in the pattern of floor surfaces, in the shapes of windows, furniture and alcoves. In addition, each of the three floors has its own colour scheme: blue and yellow (sea and sand) for the ground floor, green (landscape) for the middle, and pink, orange and red (buildings) for the top. The overall effect is warm, vibrant yet restful, pleasingly coherent while avoiding uniformity.

As you walk through the hospital, you come across many paintings, murals and prints of a notably high standard. These too reflect the world of the island, both in their content and by virtue of having been commissioned from local artists and groups. A bold community embroidery, based on a design by Candace Bahouth and showing sea-life off the Needles, hangs above the stairs in the reception area. In the outpatients area there are pieces of artwork incorporating postcard-style messages from the island's principal towns, and poems with local connections - some Tennyson, and Keats's 'Ode to a Nightingale', written in Ventnor. Upstairs near a ward entrance, work by the local quilters' group and embroiderers' guild focuses on the island's history and topography. And on a specially built curved wall at the entrance to the children's unit, a large, colourful and arresting mural by Brian Chapman depicts aspects of the island's coastline.

Guy Eades believes artwork of this kind has a very positive impact. 'Some modern hospitals have gone for the "hotel feel" - efficient but depersonalised,' he says. 'We try to avoid that, and bring in the local community to get the individual feel. I think that's what makes it a healing environment.'

As we pause to look at some strikingly beautiful examples of calligraphy in the consultation and examination rooms, a passing nurse expresses her dislike of one of them. Art being such a subjective matter, such a reaction is hardly surprising. 'The whole point of artists is that they stimulate reactions, and that may be unpredictable,' Guy Eades says. 'We're not just trying to produce a comfy statement in favour of the status quo.'

Needless to say, there have been difficulties over questions of artistic taste. One of these arose over the question of the design for the curtains to go round patients' beds. Some of the ward sisters were less than happy with the fact that they no longer had the chance to make an individual choice; others disliked the designs that were being proposed. The process of consultation was long-drawn out, and at times acrimonious.

'There are tough dilemmas when you're consulting,' says John Bird. 'How far does democracy go? We didn't want to lose the sisters' goodwill, but on the other hand we felt we'd given it a good airing, and that our choice of design would work. Sometimes you have to take decisions because you think you've got it right. Now individual sisters will tell you they've got the best curtains; they're proud of them.'

Consultation has nevertheless been a key feature of the design process. Ideas for introducing the arts into the daily life of the hospital have been sought from a wide variety of sources - not just from artists and interior designers, but also nurses, doctors and consultants, managers and, importantly, patients.

As a result, St Mary's now has a wide-ranging arts programme which includes visits from outside groups and individuals. Activities include recitals, dance and theatre performances, poetry and story-telling sessions, which are held in the day rooms attached to the wards. Guy Eades believes that the benefits of such visits are not just on one side: 'I think artists need to know more about what goes on in hospitals,' he says.

Patient involvement in the arts is seen as a priority, and many of the visiting professional artists use participation as a normal element in their work. In addition, patients who have a particular activity they want to pursue, such as painting, patchwork or embroidery, can be given the facilities to do so.

Guy Eades stresses the importance of having the support of nursing and medical staff for such activities. While the arts are now seen as a normal part of hospital life at St Mary's, the wishes of individual departments still have to be met. Recently a story-telling group wanted to work in the children's unit, but staff there felt they wanted to do the story-telling themselves. 'Their judgement had to be respected,' Guy Eades says. 'You can only go as far as people want to go.'

It's also clearly important to be sensitive to the needs of particular groups of patients, by ensuring that the arts activity is an appropriate one. This can be more difficult to get right when it comes to, say, a

Left *The main entrance foyer of St Mary's, with Candace Bahouth's tapestry 'Sea Life off the Needles' in the background.*

Below *The artist supervises the tapestry-making.*

Bottom *The tapestry.*

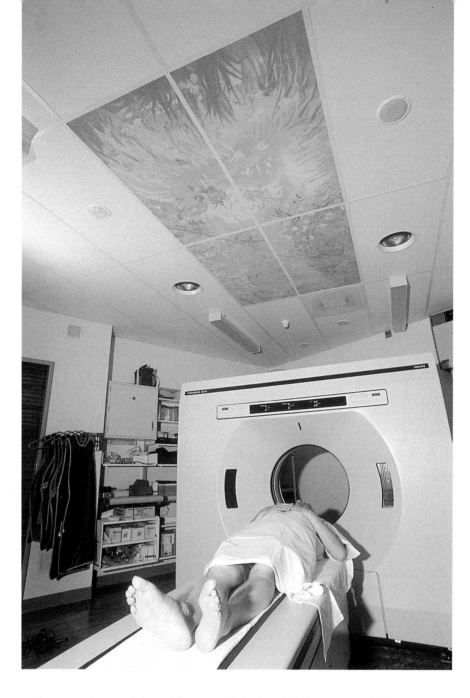

High art: a patient in the body-scanner room contemplates Anne Toms' painting.

performance in one of the public areas of the hospital. A recent recital by a chamber group in one corner of the reception area did not meet with universal approval, principally it seems because of the group's choice of early classical music rather than popular tunes.

The funding for all these initiatives has come from a multiplicity of sources, including private sponsorship. Despite the vision of the overall design concept, some features - such as the internal courtyards - had to be fiercely fought for as budgets came under scrutiny. Some of the landscaping projects outside the building did in fact get axed, which meant that money had to be raised from a private sponsor. This explains the ugly, sprawling car park at the front of the building.

'That wouldn't have been allowed in any other kind of planning,' Guy Eades says. 'The importance of landscape is still undervalued, so the budget has been used as a contingency one for other people's failures. When you're designing a healing environment, that's not good enough. There's still a long way to go to change attitudes.'

Nevertheless, the overall attitude to the present arts provision at St Mary's does represent a breakthrough. The hospital has just agreed a four-year business plan for Healing Arts, which moves the core administration costs away from charitable trusts, so that by 1995/96 they will assume the funding responsibilities together with the Community Health Services. John Bird sees this as a significant development. 'Services now see the arts as essential,' he says. 'They're seen both as cost-effective, and as providing the type of service they want to deliver.'

This belief is much in evidence around the island, in all its hospitals, health centres and clinics. One of the many centres to benefit has been the Frank James Community Hospital in East Cowes. The hospital's use of artists in fact pre-dates the advent of the new project, but its programme is now more varied, and the organisation of activities properly coordinated with those taking place elsewhere on the island.

The patients, all of whom are elderly, have weekly reminiscence therapy classes in the hospital, using art and music. But they also have contact with many outside artists. Recent activities include a performance of Chekhov by local schools, workshops with members of the Bournemouth Philharmonic, a visit from the Forest Forge Theatre Group, a presentation by a dance group, and a musical extravaganza. One particularly popular event was the performance by the small opera company Connaught Opera of songs from old films and shows, which involved the singers holding the hands of individual patients, and singing their favourite songs to them.

Chris Hart, sister in charge, says she'd hate to be without the arts service. 'It helps the patients tremendously, gives them something to look forward to,' she says. 'It brings them out of their shells, especially when you're hard pressed to find the

Brian Chapman's arresting mural picks out aspects of the Island's coastline.

time to be with them much. Some of them don't communicate a lot, but they'll paint the most beautiful pictures.' She admits that the choice of visiting artists has occasionally taken her by surprise. 'I wouldn't have thought the patients would have been keen on *Gulliver's Travels* in mime, but to my surprise they loved it.'

The Cowes hospital, like all the other health care institutions on the island, has access to Healing Arts' extensive collection of paintings, now totalling around 900. These can be borrowed, and changed when wanted. 'In the old days we would have just gone out and chosen some reproductions pictures and put them on the wall,' Chris Hart recalls. 'Now we have original paintings, drawings and prints by artists.' She admits that the staff don't always agree about the pictures: 'But at least they cause discussion and debate.'

Some of the pictures on the wall at the St Cross Day Centre in Newport are done by the handicapped patients themselves. Art here is one of the main activities, as assistant manager Carol Laidler explains: 'Their paintings and sketches usually reflect their feelings, so someone might do a beautiful drawing, and then nothing for a month.'

St Mary's chapel with furniture designed by Rod Wales, and inscription by Andrew Mead.

The centre has twice-weekly sessions from the musicians of Independent Arts, who have helped some of the more profoundly handicapped patients to hold and use percussion instruments. Recently they've had visits from the dance theatre group Common Ground and Connaught Opera, and arts workshops by Sarajan Creativity from India, all of which went down well. 'Music is the greatest asset for the patients,' Carol Laidler says. 'Everyone can get involved, even if it's just clapping. Drama is often not as successful, their imagination is limited, they can't pretend.'

Porters driving past 'The Spine of the Wight' by Alan McPherson.

She and other staff at the centre work closely with Guy Eades, and clearly find his varied arts programme of immense value, both to patients and themselves. 'It's amazing what people will do with strangers, when you think they aren't going to do anything. People come in with such different ideas, whereas working here all the time you can't help getting a bit stale.'

The island has also been innovatory on another score, being the first health authority to employ a writer on a year's full-time residency. Writer Fiona Sampson spent 1988/89 working with patients in various hospitals and day centres, encouraging them to express their thoughts and feelings through writing, with the aim of providing a positive experience, increasing self-confidence and reducing stress. (See page 63 for a more detailed account of her residency.)

The ambitious arts programme in the authority has been a pioneering one in all kinds of ways. St Mary's itself is a good example of how fruitful and productive genuine partnership can be. As Guy Eades says about its conception: 'It's really worked, but only because everyone has respected each other's role and professional abilities.' The hospital has already become a model for future health provision, in which colour, beauty, humour and creative spirit are reflected through the arts to provide an uplifting experience for all hospital users.

Chapter 8
A Manifesto for Action

'Everyone has the right freely to participate in the cultural life of the community, to enjoy the arts, and to share in scientific advancement and its benefits.'

Article 27, UN Universal Declaration of Human Rights, 1985

Slowly, the argument about the healing power of the arts has begun to be considered more widely, as arts projects and programmes have made their impact, and begun to affect the way health managers think about improving the quality of life for their patients. Yet until such a notion is sufficiently accepted to be taken into the mainstream of health care, such efforts will continue to be piecemeal, have to be argued from scratch, and be vulnerable to changes of personnel and budget cuts. Although very few countries have gone as far as the UK in recognising the enormous value of the arts in health care, this recognition is still too dependent on the vision and determination of a few individuals. Many have had to struggle ceaselessly and in isolation to establish a role for the arts, in the face of inertia, unnecessary bureaucracy, poor resources, or simply a lack of imagination.

If we believe that people should have the right of access to the arts regardless of illness, handicap or disability, the question then arises, how is this to be achieved? What is needed, if the movement that began 20 years ago is not to falter, is a Manifesto for Action, that builds on the recommendations made by the Attenborough Committee in 1985. There is little doubt that the 12 points of the manifesto outlined here would command widespread support.

The first three recommendations were in essence also made by the Attenborough Committee in 1985. Since they have not been implemented on a national basis, they need to be re-stated. The other nine focus on the need for more information about where the arts are being used and what effect they are having, better training both for health care staff and artists, more opportunities for patients living in the community, and a greater role for the arts in settings other than hospitals.

The manifesto

● All those with responsibility for health care services should be required to develop the use of the arts, and to establish programmes which use the services of artists in all kinds of health care settings.

● All health authorities should appoint an arts coordinator to develop relevant arts programmes within their area of authority.

● The capital cost for any new health care building or redevelopment should include a percentage, preferably a 1% minimum, allocated for the provision of artworks and facilities for arts activities.

● A national arts in health care audit should be carried out, in order to identify the main gaps in provision, at national, regional and district level. The audit should be funded by the Department of Health, and a copy of the results made available to all relevant health care and arts organisations.

● A register of artists willing and able to work in the health care field should be compiled for each region by the regional arts boards, and made available to all health care institutions in that region.

● All health care venues, including health centres and GPs' surgeries, should consider what role the arts could play in the service they offer to their patients, and put their conclusions out for consultation to their local community.

● Research should be commissioned to provide proper scientific evidence of how the quality of life of patients in receipt of health care is improved by contact with the arts, and how such contact affects rates of recovery, use of medical resources, and other kinds of behaviour.

● The use of the arts in health care should become part of the education and training of health care staff such as doctors and nurses, as well as health managers. In-service courses for such staff on the use of particular art-forms should be much more widely available.

● Short courses should be set up for artists wishing to be employed in this field, to acquaint them with the practicalities of the work, and help them to develop the necessary personal and communication skills to carry it out effectively.

● Training for musicians, actors and other performers should include experience in performing in community settings, including health care institutions, on the lines of the course run at the Guildhall School of Music and Drama in London.

● Minimum rates of pay should be agreed for all artists working in health care, to avoid exploitation, and to encourage the involvement of the widest possible range of artists.

● Health authorities should, with other bodies, set up arts centres or art studios in their local communities along the lines of the START project in Manchester and the Art Studio in Sunderland, for use by patients living in the community.

If these recommendations were implemented, the social, spiritual and medical benefits to patients and health care staff would be considerable, and unmistakable.

The way ahead

In a civilised society where the importance of culture is recognised, the value of such a policy would be self-evident. In the UK, where culture is all too often seen as separate from life itself, we badly need to get away from the surgeon/barber institutionalised vision of health care, and acknowledge the potential of the holistic approach. There is an urgent need to develop far-sighted cultural policies for health. Such a policy ties in with the growing interest in and use of complementary medicine, and the holistic approach which aims to cure the whole person, rather than simply deal with their physical symptoms. One project outside the UK provides an excellent model. In 1989 the Wanganui Health Board, responsible for the Waikato Hospital, New Zealand, stated: 'The board recognises its responsibility to support creative expression and cultural improvement as a necessary and integral part of our holistic health care service, and believes it is of importance to define the many roles in which the arts can be used as tools for creativity and communication.' The board then emphasises: 'Such a policy does not stand alone as a separate and different piece of policy; it should be integrated into the overall strategic plan.'

Such an approach to the use of the arts in health care requires vision, understanding and commitment, as well as leadership and support in the political sphere. At government level in the UK there is an increasing awareness of this kind of work, though whether its importance is understood is another question. All ministers ally themselves to the work, because it is not the kind of activity anyone would oppose in principle. But in order for there to be greater commitment, in resources as well as moral support, a great deal of hard and persistent lobbying needs to be done at all levels.

Fortunately, there is now a handful of examples of innovative practice to provide us with valuable signposts for the future. In particular, the work done within the Isle of Wight in the last few years, and the successful integration of the arts there into the new St Mary's Hospital in Newport and into the health authority as a whole, show how a genuine partnership between planners, health care staff and arts providers can transform the quality of life for a significant number of patients. The endorsement of the work of START by the NHS Advisory Committee Inspectorate is further evidence of highly effective practice which should be replicated.

With so much activity going on, it is inevitable that standards have varied from project to project. As we have shown, there can be many reasons for a project failing to fulfil its potential. Much depends on the skills and imagination of the artists or arts coordinators concerned. But it is also important for such work to be properly funded and managed if the work is to be of a consistently high quality. Ultimately, the arts in health care should be judged in the same way as the arts are in other settings.

It has become a truism to say that the culture of the health service in the UK is changing. The opportunity is now there to ensure that the arts play a central part in the development of health care at this moment of radical change. We now have a substantial range of experience to show how the use of the arts can bring about a significant improvement in the quality of life of all concerned, and so play an important part in the healing process.

Arts Organisations

Arts Councils

Arts Council of Great Britain
14 Great Peter Street,
London SW1P 3NQ
Tel. 071-333 0100

Scottish Arts Council
12 Manor Place, Edinburgh EH3 7DD
Tel. 031-226 6051

Welsh Arts Council
Holst House, Museum Place,
Cardiff CF1 3NX
Tel. 0222 394711

Regional Arts Boards

Eastern Arts Board
Cherry Hinton Hall, Cherry Hinton Road,
Cambridge CB1 4DW
Tel. 0223 215355

East Midlands Arts Board
Mountfields House, Forest Road,
Loughborough, Leicestershire
LE11 3HU
Tel. 0509 218292

London Arts Board
Elme House, 133 Long Acre,
London WC2E 9AF
Tel. 071-240 1313

Northern Arts Board
9-10 Osborne Terrace, Jesmond,
Newcastle-upon-Tyne NE2 1NZ
Tel. 091-281 6334

North West Arts Board
12 Harter Street, Manchester M1 6HY
Tel. 061-228 3062

Southern Arts Board
13 St Clement Street,
Winchester SO23 9DQ
Tel. 0962 855099

South East Arts Board
Bradninch Place, Gandy Street,
Exeter EX4 3LS
Tel. 0392 218188

West Midlands Arts Board
82 Granville Street, Birmingham B1 2LH
Tel. 021-631 3121

Yorkshire and Humberside Arts Board
21 Bond Street, Dewsbury WF13 1AX
Tel. 0924 455555

Regional Arts Associations in Wales

North Wales Arts Association
10 Wellfield House, Bangor,
Gwynedd LL57 1ER
Tel. 0248 351077

South East Wales Arts Association
Victoria Street, Cwmbran,
Gwent NP44 3YT
Tel. 0633 875075

West Wales Arts
3 Red Street, Carmarthen,
Dyfed SA31 1QL
Tel. 0267 234248

The SHAPE and Artlink Network

Artability South East
St James Centre, Quarry Road,
Tunbrige Wells, Kent TN1 2EY
Tel. 0892 515478

Artlink Central
The Norman MacEwan Centre,
Cameronian Street, Stirling FK8 2DX
Tel. 0786 50971

Artlink East
Unit 2, Peterborough Arts Centre,
Orton Goldhay, Peterborough PE2 0JQ
Tel. 0733 237073

Artlink Edinburgh and the Lothians
13a Spittal Street, Edinburgh EH3 9DY
Tel. 031-229 3555

Artlink for Lincolnshire and Humberside
c/o Humberside Leisure Service,
Central Library, Albion Street,
Hull HU1 3TF
Tel. 0482 224040

Artlink West Midlands
The Garage Arts and Media Centre,
1 Hatherton Street, Walsall WS1 1YB
Tel. 0922 616566

Artlink West Yorkshire
(previously Shape Up North)
191 Bellevue Road, Leeds LS3 1HG
Tel. 0532 431005

Arts Connection
(previously Solent Artlink)
Cumberland Centre, Reginald Road,
Portsmouth, Hampshire PO4 9HN
Tel. 0705 828392

Artshare South West
c/o South West Arts, Bradninch Place,
Gandy Street, Exeter EX4 3HA
Tel. 0392 218923

Arts Integration Merseyside
Mount Vernon Green, Hall Lane,
Liverpool L7 8TF
Tel. 051-709 0990

East Midlands Shape
27a Belvoir Street, Leicester LE1 6SL
Tel. 0533 552933

Northern Shape
Todd's Nook Centre, Monday Crescent,
Newcastle-upon-Tyne NE1 1PG
Tel. 091-226 0701

North West Shape
The Green Prefab, Back of Shawgrove
School, Cavendish Road,
West Didsbury, Manchester M20 8JR
Tel. 061-434 8666

Shape Buckinghamshire
38b Princes Estate, Summerleys Road,
Princes Risborough, Buckinghamshire
HP17 9PX
Tel. 0844 274493

Shape London
1 Thorpe Close, London W10 5XL
Tel. 081-960 9245

Southern Artlink (now Ithaca)
Unit 4, St John Fisher School,
Sandy Lane West, Oxford OX4 5LD
Tel. 0865 714652

Other Organisations

Age Exchange Theatre Trust
The Reminiscence Centre,
11 Blackheath Village, London SE3 9LA
Tel. 081-318 9105

Art in Partnership
233 Cowgate, Edinburgh EH1 1NQ
Tel. 031-225 4463

Artistic Licence
23 Eton Grove, Wollaton Park,
Nottingham NG8 1FT
Tel. 0602 282310

Artists' Agency
First and Second Floor,
18 Norfolk Street, Sunderland,
Tyne and Wear SR1 1EA
Tel. 091-510 9318

ArtsCare
25 Adelaide Street, Belfast BT2 8FH
Tel. 0232 324431

Arts for Health
Manchester Metropolitan University,
All Saints, Oxford Road,
Manchester M15 6BY
Tel. 061-236 8916

Bedside Manners Theatre Company
Highgate Newtown Community Centre,
25 Bertram Street, London N19 5DQ
Tel. 071-282 2526

Bellarmine Hospital Arts Project
Kirklands Hospital, Fallside Road,
Bothwell, Glasgow G71 8BB
Tel. 0698 852508

British Health Care Arts
Duncan of Jordanstone College of Art,
Perth Road, Dundee, Scotland DD1 4HT
Tel. 0382 23261

Carnegie UK Trust
Comely Park House, Dunfermline, Fife,
Scotland KY12 7EJ
Tel. 0383 721445

Carousel Project
2 St George's Place, Brighton,
Sussex BN1 4GB
Tel. 0273 570840

Celebratory Arts for Primary Health Care
32/34 Main Street, High Bentham,
Lancaster LA2 7HN
Tel. 05242 62672

Centre for Accessible Environments
35 Great Smith Street,
London SW1P 3BJ
Tel. 071-222 7980

Common Ground Sign Dance Theatre
Hanwell Community Centre,
Westcott Crescent, London W7 1PD
Tel. 081-575 1078

Community Music
Interchange Studios, Dalby Street,
London NW5 3NQ
Tel. 071-485 8553

Conquest: The Society for Art for
Physically Handicapped People
3 Beverley Close, East Ewell, Epsom,
Surrey KT17 3HB
Tel. 081-393 6102

Council for Music in Hospitals
74 Queen's Road, Hersham,
Surrey KT12 5LW
Tel. 0932 252809
(Scottish Office)
10 Forth Street, Edinburgh EH1 3LD
Tel. 031-556 5848

English Touring Opera
121 Westminster Business Square,
Durham Street, London SE11 5JH
Tel. 071-820 1131/1141

Framework Community Theatre
Unit 102a, Oyston Mill, Strand Road,
Preston PR1 8UR
Tel. 0772 735082

Hospice Arts
c/o Forbes House, 9 Artillery Lane,
London E1 7LP
Tel. 0245 358130

Hospital Arts Manchester
The Arts Centre, St Mary's Hospital,
Hathersage Road, Manchester M13 0JH
Tel. 061-256 4389

Jabadao
29 Queens Road, Bradford BD8 7BS
Tel. 0274 547274

King Edward's Hospital Fund for London
14 Palace Court, London W2 4HT
Tel. 071-727 0581

Live Music Now!
15 Grosvenor Gardens,
London SW1 0BD
Tel. 071-828 7073
(Scottish Office)
14 Lennox Street,
Edinburgh EH4 1QA
Tel. 031-332 6356
(Welsh Office)
1 Miles Court, Gwaelod y Garth,
Cardiff CF4 8SR
Tel. 0222 813691

Living Memory Theatre
36 Lime Street,
Newcastle-upon-Tyne NE1 2PN
Tel. 091-261 1031

Ludus Dance Company
Ludus Dance Centre, Assembly Rooms,
King Street, Lancaster LA1 1RE
Tel. 0524 35936

National Music and Disability
Information Service
Dartington College of Arts, Totnes,
Devon TQ9 6EJ
Tel. 0803 866701

Paintings in Hospitals
c/o Samaritan Hospital,
Marylebone Road, London NW1 5YE
Tel. 071-723 7422
(Scottish Office)
10 Forth Street, Edinburgh EH1 3LD
Tel. 031-557 3490

Paintings in Hospitals Hospice Scheme
c/o Paintings in Hospitals,
Samaritan Hospital, Marylebone Road,
London NW1 5YE
Tel. 071-723 7422

Prism Theatre
Packhorse Lane, English Street,
Carlisle CA3 8JP
Tel. 0228 819989

Project Ability
18 Albion Street, Glasgow G1 1LH
Tel. 041-552 2822

Proper Job Theatre Company
48a Byram Arcade, Westgate,
Huddersfield, West Yorkshire HD1 1AD
Tel. 0484 514687

Public Art Commissions Agency
Studio 6, Victoria Works,
Vittoria Street, Birmingham B1 3PE
Tel. 021-212 4454

Public Art Development Trust
1a Cobham Mews, Agar Grove,
London NW1 9SB
Tel. 071-284 4983

Royal Opera House
Floral Street, Covent Garden,
London WC2E 9DD
Tel. 071-240 1200

St Mary's Hospital
Healing Arts Department
Parkhurst, Newport,
Isle of Wight PO30 5TG
Tel. 0983 524081

Dr Malcolm Rigler
Withymoor Surgery Arts Project
Turners Lane, Brierley Hill,
Dudley DY5 2PG
Tel. 0384 73670

Further Reading

Books

Alexander, Lynne (ed), *Now I Can Tell: Poems from St John's Hospice*, Macmillan, 1990.

Art in New Zealand Hospitals, Queen Elizabeth II Arts Council,1992.

Artists and Art Therapists: A Brief Discussion of their Roles within Hospitals, Clinics, Special Schools and in the Community, Carnegie UK Trust.

Arts Council of Great Britain, *Arts and Disability Directory: Off the Shelf and Into Action*, ACGB, 1991.

Berry, Judy, *Arts in Health Care: First Step for Managers*, Yorkshire Arts, 1991.

Braden, Su, *Artists and People*, Routledge & Kegan Paul, 1978.

Carnegie Council, *Arts and Disabled People: The Attenborough Report*, Bedford Square Press, 1985.

Carnegie Council, *After Attenborough: Arts and Disabled People*, Bedford Square Press, 1988.

Coles, Peter, *Art in the National Health*, Department of Health and Social Security, 1983.

Coles, Peter, *Manchester Hospitals' Arts Project*, Calouste Gulbenkian Foundation, 1981.

Coles, Peter, *The Arts in a Health District*, Department of Health and Social Security, 1985.

Cox, Murray (ed), *Shakespeare Comes to Broadmoor: The Performance of Tragedy in a Secure Psychiatric Hospital*, Jessica Kingsley, 1992.

Crimmin, Michaela, Shand, William S, Thomas, Jenny A, *The Art of Dying: The Story of Two Sculptors' Residency in a Hospice*, King Edward's Hospital Fund for London/The Forbes Trust, 1989.

Eisenhauer, Jane, *Travellers' Tales: Poetry from a Hospice*, Marshall Pickering, 1990.

Gittins, Chrissie (ed), *Somebody Said That Word: Living in a Hospice*, Littlewood Arc, 1991.

Goodenough, Simon (ed), *Art Ability: Fifty Creative People Talk About Ability and Disability*, Michael Russsell, 1989.

Greene, Lesley, *Art in Hospitals: A Guide*, King's Fund, 1989.

Hague, Ian, and Barnett, Jenny, *The Arts and Terminal Care: First Step for Managers*, Yorkshire Arts, 1991.

Levete, Gina, *The Creative Tree: Active Participation in the Arts for People who are Disadvantaged*, Michael Russell, 1987.

Lord, Geoffrey (ed), *The Arts and Disabilities*, MacDonald, 1981.

Lowe, Nicholas, and McMillan, Michael, *Living Proof: Views of a World Living with HIV and AIDS*, Artists' Agency, 1992.

McCabe, Mary and McVicar, Ewan, *Streets, Schemes and Stages: Social Work's Year of the Arts*, Strathclyde Regional Council, 1991.

Miles, Malcolm (ed), *Art and Mental Health Hospitals: Art as an Effective Element in the Care of the Mentally Ill and Mentally Handicapped*, British Health Care Arts, 1991.

Miles, Malcolm, *Artists in Residence in Hospitals: The Contributions of Artists to the Quality of Life in Acute and Long-Stay Hospitals*, British Health Care Arts, 1991.

Moss, Linda, *Art for Health's Sake*, Carnegie UK Trust, 1987.

Moss, Linda, *Art and Healthcare*, Department of Health and Social Security, 1988.

Payne, Helen (ed), *Arts in Healthcare in the Northern Region*, Northern Arts, 1992.

Pearson, Anne, *Arts for Everyone: Guidance on Provision for Disabled People*, Carnegie UK Trust and Centre for Accessible Environments, 1985.

Sampson, Fiona, *Writing in Health Care, Healing Arts: Isle of Wight*, 1989.

Scher, Peter, *Environmental Design Quality in Health Care*, Arts for Health, 1992.

Sim, Roger, *Looking Forward to Looking Back: Guidelines on Reminiscence and the Arts in the Care of the Elderly*, Reminiscence Project, Manchester, 1991.

Townsend, Peter (ed), *Art Within Reach: Artists and Craftworkers, Architects and Patrons in the Making of Public Art*, Thames & Hudson, 1984.

Conference reports

A Vision of Caring Environments, Arts for Health, 1989.

Music for Life: Proceedings from a Conference on Aspects of Music in Continuing and Terminal Care, British Society for Music Therapy/National Music and Disability Information Service, 1991.

References

1 Introduction

1. Speech at conference on 'A Vision of Caring Environments', Manchester, 2/3 November 1989.

2. *Capitalising on Creativity,* Trent Regional Health Authority, 1991.

3. *Notes on Nursing*, 1859, p.33.

4. *A Vision of Britain*, Doubleday, 1989, p.117.

5. See note 1.

6. 'View from a window may influence recovery from surgery', *Science*, April 1984, p.420.

7. See note 1.

2 Birth of a Movement

1. *Manchester Hospitals' Arts Project*, Calouste Gulbenkian Foundation, 1981, p.35.

2. *The Arts in a Health District*, DHSS, 1985.

3. *Arts and Disabled People: The Attenborough Report*, Bedford Square Press, 1985, p.xiii.

4. DHSS, Building Note 1.

5. Carnegie Council, *After Attenborough: Arts and Disabled People*, Bedford Square Press, 1988, p.38.

3 The Visual Environment

1. Speech at conference on 'A Vision of Caring Environments', Manchester, 2/3 November 1989.

2. *The Independent*, 23 June 1992.

3. See note 1.

4. Letter to the authors.

5. Speech at conference on 'Creating Health Care Environments', King's Fund Centre, London, April 1992.

6. *Arts Extra*, Mid Sussex arts newsletter, spring 1991.

7. *Art Within Reach*, edited by Peter Townsend, Thames & Hudson, 1984, p.42.

8. Letter to authors.

9. Letter to authors.

10. *Art Within Reach*, p.57.

11. Letter to authors.

12. *Evaluating Art in Hospitals*, Valerie Holman, British Health Care Arts, forthcoming.

13. *Arts in Healthcare in the Northern Region*, edited by Helen Payne, Northern Arts, 1992, p.11.

14. 'Creativity produces healing', *Artery*, Arts for Health magazine, no.3, summer 1991, p.6.

15. Hospital Arts, 'Annual Report 1989-90', p.9.

16. Ibid, p.2.

17. Letter to authors.

18. *The Art of Dying: The Story of Two Sculptors' Residency in a Hospice*, Michaela Crimmin, William S Shand and Jenny A Thomas, King Edward's Hospital Fund for London/ The Forbes Trust, 1989.

19. 'An area of risk,' *Artery,* no.3, summer 1991, p.6.

20. See note 1.

21. Information sent to authors.

22. 'New mural for Princess Hospital', *Artery,* no.4, autumn 1991, p.6.

4 Working Together

1. Letter to authors.

2. Booklet on the hospital's art project.

3. Letter to authors.

4. Interim report, January 1991.

5. Ibid.

6. Interim report, October 1991.

7. Letter to authors.

8. Letter to authors.

9. Letters to authors.

10. 'Painting a healthy picture', *Women's Art*, July/August 1992, p.14.

11. Letter to authors.

12. 'Linking patients with the world of art', *The Gazette*, 9 November 1991, p.1034.

13. Letter to authors.

14. Artist's report on the residency, 1990/91.

15. Letter to authors.

16. Letter to authors.

17. Booklet on 'Illumined Shadows' exhibition, Darlington Arts Centre, 10 March-21 April 1990.

18. Case-study sheet, Artists' Agency, 1990.

19. Interview with Jonathan Croall.

5 Music, Dance and Drama

1. See Linda Moss, *Art for Health's Sake*, Carnegie UK Trust, 1987, p.20.

2. Letter to authors.

3. Video on the work of the Council for Music in Hospitals.

4. Letter to authors.

5. 'You need more than a good performance', *Classical Music*, 21 September 1991, p.19.

6. See note 3.

7. See note 4.

8. Conversation with Jonathan Croall.

9. Letter to authors.

10. *Arts in Healthcare in the Northern Region*, p.8.

11. *Hospice Care*, no.11, Northern Ireland, spring 1992.

12. Internal report, Ludus Dance Company.

13. Final report on project, May 1992.

14. Letter to authors.

15. Conversation with Jonathan Croall.

16. Letter to authors.

17. Letter to authors.

18. Conversation with Jonathan Croall.

19. Letter to authors.

20. Janet Watts, 'King Lear Goes to Broadmoor', *Observer*, 16 February 1992.

6 Writing and Reminiscence

1. 'Why Write?', *Artery,* no.4, autumn 1991, p.5.

2. *Writing in Health Care*, report on the Isle of Wight residency, 1989, p.30.

3. Letter to authors.

4. Letter to authors.

5. Letter to authors.

6. Interim report on Milestone House arts programme, Artlink, 1991.

7. *Streets, Schemes and Stages*, edited by Mary McCabe and Ewan McVicar, Strathclyde Regional Council, 1991, p.188.

8. See note 3.

9. Interview with Jonathan Croall.

10. See note 3.

11. See note 4.

12. *Writing in Health Care*, p.35.

Credits for Illustrations

3
Dept of Medical Illustration, St Bartholomew's Hospital

4
Christopher Barrett

5
The Royal London Hospital Archives & Museum (top)
Ron Davies (bottom)

6
Steve Shrimpton, Teaching Media Unit, Southampton University

11
Brian Chapman (top)
Helen Kitchen, Hospital Arts (bottom)

15
Cover illustration Marcus Ward

17-20
Helen Kitchen, Hospital Arts

21
Helen Kitchen, Hospital Arts (top and bottom)
Brian Chapman (middle)

22
Helen Kitchen, Hospital Arts

23
Daily Mail

25
Faye Carey

26
Hospital Arts

27
Barrie Stead

28
Barrie Stead (top)
Steve Yates, Arts for Health (bottom)

29
Medical Illustration, Aberdeen Royal Infirmary (top)
Steve Yates, Arts for Health (bottom)

30
Cartoon by Honeysett

31
Steve Yates, Arts for Health
Prudence Cuming Associates Ltd (inset)

32
Graham Crowley

33
Helen Kitchen, Hospital Arts

34
Ardmore Advertising and Promotion (top)
Camilla Jessel (bottom)

35
Lance Browne

37
Steve Yates, Arts for Health

42
Pam Sandals (left)
Keith Pattison (right)

44
Jack Sutton, Snaps (left)
Hospital Arts (right)

45
Rose Pickering

48-51
Bellarmine Arts

54
Steve Yates, Arts for Health

55-56
Keith Pattison

57
T Bailey Forman Newspapers Ltd (left)
Visuals Photography (right)

58
Dee Conway

59
C L Stroud

61
Ian Christy (top)
Neil Libbert (bottom)

67-68
Helen Kitchen, Hospital Arts

71-75
Postcards by Celebratory Arts

72
Malcolm Rigler

74
Paul France

85
June Badger

86
Steve Yates, Arts for Health

87
Steve Shrimpton, Teaching Media Unit, Southampton University (top)
Steve Yates, Arts for Health (bottom)

88-91
Steve Yates, Arts for Health

Index